The Workbook on Becoming Alive in Christ

The Workbook on Becoming Alive in Christ

Maxie Dunnam

UPPER ROOM BOOKS®
NASHVILLE

The Workbook on Becoming Alive in Christ

The Upper Room® Website: http://www.upperroom.org

Photo credits (in order of appearance)—Dennis Mansell; Steve Takatsuno; Barry Edmonds/CORN'S PHOTO SERVICE; David S. Strickler/STRIX PIX; David Mansell; Bob Taylor; David S. Strickler/STRIX PIX.

Book and Cover Design: John Robinson
Cover Transparency: Frances Dorris
Seventh Printing: 2000
ISBN 0-8358-0542-5

Contents

Introduction 7

The Plan 8

Sharing with Others 10

Suggestions for Initial Get-Acquainted Meeting 12

1. The Indwelling Christ

Daily Guides 15

Group Meeting for Week One..35

2. Dying and Rising with Christ

Daily Guides 39

Group Meeting for Week Two..58

3. An Affirming Presence

Daily Guides 63

Group Meeting for Week Three 80

4. A Forgiving and Healing Presence

Daily Guides 85

Group Meeting for Week Four 107

5. A Guiding and Creating Presence
Daily Guides 111
Group Meeting for Week Five.....................................130

6. A Converting Presence
Daily Guides 133
Group Meeting for Week Six 150

7. Being Christ
Daily Guides 153
Group Meeting for Week Seven 169

Notes 172

Introduction

The primary focus of this workbook is *being alive in Christ*. The content is based on my book *Alive in Christ: The Dynamic Process of Spiritual Formation*. In fact, some of the content is directly quoted from that book and will be indented and followed by the abbreviation *AC* and the appropriate page number in *Alive in Christ*.

Alive in Christ was published in 1983. Since its publication, many persons have expressed their disappointment in the fact that I had not prepared the book in the workbook format of my widely used *Workbook of Living Prayer, Workbook of Intercessory Prayer,* and *Workbook on Spiritual Disciplines*. When I wrote *Alive in Christ,* I wanted to make a contribution to the growing concern for spiritual formation in Protestant Christianity which was a primary interest of mine during my ten years of ministry with *The Upper Room*.

There is a sense in which this book is the expression of the core of my theology and the call upon my life as a Christian. I believe there are two central experiential concepts in Christian theology: one, justification by grace through faith which is our theology of salvation; and two, *a person in Christ* which defines the nature and source of power for Christian living. Justification by grace through faith has always been central, especially to Protestant and/or evangelical Christianity. Yet, this second concept—the understanding of Christian living as persons being "alive in Christ"—has been grossly ignored. For that reason we have anemic expressions of Christianity. We have reduced the faith to a dry belief system, doctrinal statements to which we ascribe and creeds that we repeat rotely but do not affirm experientially. The radical notion of New Testament Christianity is that the presence of God in Jesus Christ is to be experienced not only on occasion, but the indwelling Christ is to become the shaping power of our lives. What Christ has been and done for us, we are to be and do for others.

7

This is what spiritual formation is all about. The process of spiritual formation is the process of learning to say yes to Christ every day in every way. For that reason, a workbook style for the core content of *Alive in Christ* is appropriate. Spiritual formation requires discipline, practiced effort on our part to recognize, cultivate awareness of, and give expression to the indwelling Christ.

Many have a vision of what a spiritual person ought to look like, think like, and talk like. These models usually grow out of rigid definitions of piety and stereotypes of what it means to be spiritual. I hope you will lay aside these models and come freshly to an exploration of spiritual formation.

As I contended in *The Workbook on Spiritual Disciplines,* discipline is an absolute necessity for the Christian life. We may be converted to Christ in the miracle of a moment, but becoming a saint is the task of a lifetime. And we are called to sainthood. We are to *grow up* in Christ (Eph. 4:15), to become mature in Christ (Col. 1:28), and to have the mind of Christ in us (Phil. 2:5). Paul used the metaphor of childbirth to express his groaning desire that Christians grow to the measure of the stature of the fullness of Christ. "Oh, my dear children, I feel the pangs of childbirth all over again till Christ be formed within you" (Gal. 4:19, PHILLIPS).

As Christians we do not emerge full-blown; we grow. We grow by discipline. So the purpose of the workbook is to facilitate the process of spiritual formation by providing content, ideas for reflection, and guidance for discipline in order that we might appropriate experientially the dynamic presence of the indwelling Christ.

THE PLAN

The plan for this adventure is the same as for my three previous workbooks. It calls for a seven-week commitment. It is an individual journey, but my hope is that you will share it with some fellow pilgrims who will meet together once each week during the seven weeks of the study. You are asked to give thirty minutes each day to learn about and appropriate ideas and disciplines for spiritual formation. For most persons these thirty minutes will come at the beginning of the day. However, if it is not possible for you to give the time at the beginning of the day, do it whenever the time is available—but do it regularly. The purpose of this spiritual journey must not be forgotten: to incorporate the content into your daily life.

The workbook is arranged in seven major divisions, each designed to guide you for one week. These divisions contain seven sections, one for each day of the week. Each day of the week will have two major aspects: reading about the discipline, and reflecting and recording.

Reading about the Discipline

In each day's section you will read something about being alive in Christ—not too much, but enough to provide something of the nature and meaning of life in Christ and possibilities of cultivating awareness and giving expression to the indwelling Christ. Included in this will be some portions of scripture. The scripture is a basic resource for Christian discipline and living. Content quoted directly from *Alive in Christ* is indented and each quote is followed by the page number where the quote can be found in that book. Quotations from sources other than scripture and *Alive in Christ* are followed by the author's name and the page number on which the quote can be found. These citations are keyed to the Notes section at the back of the workbook where you will find complete bibliographic information for each source.

Throughout the workbook you will see this symbol ✳ ✳ ✳. When you come to the symbol, *please stop*. Do not read any further. Think and reflect as you are requested to do in order to internalize the ideas being shared or the experience reflected upon.

Reflecting and Recording

Then each day, there will be a time for reflecting and recording. This dimension calls you to record some of your reflections. The degree of meaning you receive from this workbook is largely dependent upon your faithfulness to its practice. You may be unable on a particular day to do precisely what is requested. If so, then simply record that fact and make a note of why you can't follow through. This may give you insight about yourself and help you to grow.

Also, on some days there may be more suggestions than you can deal with in the time you have. Do what is most meaningful for you, and don't feel *guilty*.

The emphasis is upon growth, not perfection. Don't feel guilty if you do not follow exactly the pattern of the days. Follow the content and direction seriously, but not slavishly. Always remember that this is a personal pilgrimage. What you write in your personal workbook is your private property. You may not wish to share it with anyone. For this reason, no two people should attempt to share the same workbook. The importance of what you write is not what it may mean to someone else, but what it means to you. Writing, even if it is only brief notes or single-word reminders, helps us clarify our feelings and thinking.

The significance of the reflecting and recording dimensions will grow as you move along. Even beyond the seven-week period, you will find meaning in looking back to what you wrote on a particular day in response to a particular situation.

SHARING WITH OTHERS

In the history of Christian piety, the spiritual director or guide has been a significant person. To varying degrees most of us have had spiritual directors—persons to whom we have turned for support and direction in our spiritual pilgrimage. There is a sense in which this workbook can be a spiritual guide, for you can use it as a private venture without participating in a group.

Its meaning will be enhanced, however, if you share the adventure with eight to twelve others. In this way, the "priesthood of all believers" will come alive, and you will profit from the growing insights of others, and they will profit from yours.

John Wesley believed that "Christian conferencing" was a means of grace for Christians. By Christian conferencing he meant simply Christians sharing intentionally their Christian experience and understanding in deliberate and serious conversation. He designed the "class meeting" as a vehicle for this discipline. In such a fellowship of Christian conversation and shared life, "one loving heart sets another on fire." Your weekly gathering can be that kind of means of grace. A guide for group sharing is included in the text at the end of each week.

If this is a group venture, all persons should begin their personal involvement with the workbook on the same day, so that when you come together to share as a group all will have been dealing with the same material and will be at the same place in the text. It will be helpful if you have an initial get-acquainted group meeting to begin the adventure. A guide for this meeting is provided in this introduction.

Group sessions for this workbook are designed to last one and one-half hours (with the exception of this initial meeting). Those sharing in the group should covenant to attend all sessions unless an emergency prevents attendance. There will be seven weekly sessions following this first get-acquainted time.

A group consisting of eight to twelve members is about the right size. Larger numbers limit individual involvement.

One person can provide the leadership for the entire seven weeks, or leaders can be assigned from week to week. The leader's task:

- to read directions and determine ahead of time how to handle the session. It may not be possible to use all the suggestions for sharing and praying together. Feel free to select those you think will be most meaningful and those for which you have adequate time.

- to model a style of openness, honesty, and warmth. A leader should not ask others to share what he or she is not willing to share. Usually the leader should be the first to share, especially as it relates to personal experiences.

- to moderate the discussion.

- to encourage reluctant members to participate, and try to prevent a few persons from doing all the talking.

- to keep the sharing centered in personal experience, rather than academic debate.

- to honor the time schedule. If it appears necessary to go longer than one and one-half hours, the leader should get consensus for continuing another twenty or thirty minutes.

- to see that meeting time and place are known by all, especially if meetings are held in different homes.

- to make sure necessary materials for meetings are available and that the meeting room is arranged ahead of time.

It is desirable that weekly meetings be held in the homes of the participants. (Hosts or hostesses should make sure there are as few interruptions as possible, e.g., children, telephone, pets, etc.) If meetings are held in a church, they should be in an informal setting. Participants are asked to dress casually, to be comfortable and relaxed.

If refreshments are served, they should come after the formal meeting. In this way, those who wish to stay longer for informal discussion may do so, while those who need to keep to a specific time schedule will be free to leave, but will get the full value of the meeting time.

SUGGESTIONS FOR INITIAL GET-ACQUAINTED MEETING

Since the initial meeting is for the purpose of getting acquainted and beginning the shared pilgrimage, here is a way to get started. (If name tags are needed, provide them.)

1. Have each person in the group give his or her full name and the name by which each wishes to be called. Do away with titles. Address all persons by their first name or nickname. (Each person should make a list of the names somewhere in his/her workbook.)

2. Let each person in the group share one of the happiest, most exciting, or most meaningful experiences he/she has had during the past three or four weeks. After all persons have shared in this way, let the entire group sing the doxology ("Praise God, from Whom All Blessings Flow") or a chorus of praise.

3. After this experience of happy sharing, ask each person who will to share his/her expectations of this workbook study. Why did he or she become a part of it? What does each expect to gain from it? What are the reservations?

4. The leader should now review the introduction to the workbook and ask if there are questions about directions and procedures (this means that the leader should have read the introduction prior to the meeting). If persons have not received copies of the workbook, the books should be handed out now. *Remember that every person must have his/her own workbook.*

5. Day One in the workbook is the day following this initial meeting, and the next meeting should be held on Day Seven of the First Week. If the group must choose another weekly meeting time other than seven days from this initial session, the reading assignment should be brought in harmony with that so that the weekly meetings are always on Day Seven, and Day One is always the day following a weekly meeting.

6. Nothing binds a group together more than praying for one another. The leader should encourage each participant to write the names of each person in the group in his/her workbook, and commit to praying for them by name daily during this six weeks.

7. After checking to see that everyone knows the time and place of the next meeting, the leader may close with a prayer, thanking God for each person in the group, for the opportunity of growth, and for the possibility of growing through spiritual disciplines.

Note: If someone in the group has an instant camera, bring it to the group meeting next week. Be prepared to take a picture of each person in the group to be used as an aid to prayer.

The Indwelling Christ

Day One: *In Christ*

I myself have been made a minister of the same Gospel, and though it is true at this moment that I am suffering on behalf of you who have heard the Gospel, yet I am far from sorry about it. Indeed, I am glad, because it gives me a chance to complete in my own sufferings something of the untold pains which Christ suffers on behalf of his body, the Church. For I am a minister of the Church by divine commission, a commission granted to me for your benefit and for a special purpose: that I might fully declare God's Word—that sacred mystery which up till now has been hidden in every age and every generation, but which is now as clear as daylight to those who love God. They are those to whom God has planned to give a vision of the full wonder and splendor of his secret plan for the sons of men. And the secret is simply this: Christ *in you!* Yes, Christ *in you* bringing with him the hope of all the glorious things to come.

So, naturally, we proclaim Christ! We warn everyone we meet, and we teach everyone we can, all that we know about him, so that, if possible, we may bring every man up to his full maturity in Christ. This is what I am working at all the time, with all the strength that God gives me.

—Colossians 1:24–29, PHILLIPS

Almost every day, for four or five years now, my morning ritual has included a word to myself. Sometimes I speak it aloud, sometimes I simply register it in my awareness. Sometimes I make it a liturgy, repeating it over and over again to a breathing-in-and-out exercise, "[Maxie,] the secret is simply this: Christ *in you!* Yes, Christ *in you* bringing with him the hope of all the glorious things to come."

15

This is Phillips' translation of Colossians 1:27, addressed to me personally. If there is a growing edge in my life, and I pray God there is, it is at this point: I'm seeking and discovering the experience of the indwelling Christ. I have come to believe that this is the key to Christian experience, certainly the key to authentic Christian piety and spirituality—to be *alive in Christ* (AC, p. 13).

"In Christ" was a recurring theme for Paul, the great apostle of Jesus and the writer of this letter to the Colossians. In fact, his understanding of the Christian life revolved around two basic concepts. One, justification by faith; and two, a person in Christ. We become Christian by being justified by grace through faith. Living the Christian life means being *in Christ*. These two experiential concepts were Paul's understanding of the core Christian experience. These were the virgin springs out of which all other experiences and expressions of the Christian life flowed. During the next few days, we will explore these concepts, examining our own Christian experience in relation to them.

The primary focus of this workbook is being alive in Christ. However, we begin by focusing on justification by grace through faith. Since this is an *experiential* concept, its meaning can be plumbed only through experience. Here is the experience in the story of one person.

She was an attractive lady, barely thirty, I would guess. She came into my office smiling, a sparkle in her eyes. This was not the same person with whom I had been counseling. Something had happened. She was changed.

I had not visited with her for two or three months, but I had seen her often prior to that. I remember the first time I met her. She showed up at our church one day; none of us knew her but she asked the secretary if she could see me. I'm glad I was available. I had never seen a more nervous, anxious, uncertain person. She slumped in the chair, glancing at me only occasionally, unconsciously clenching and opening her hands. She spoke haltingly, in jerky phrases, but managed to communicate the fact that she had heard of our church's mission emphasis, particularly our work in Mexico, and she wanted to share in it. If she couldn't participate in a personal way, she'd like to contribute monthly in a financial way. The amount she mentioned seemed astronomical in relation to what I thought she must be earning.

That was the beginning of sporadic, then regular visits together. Always the elements of *doing* something, *trying* harder, *giving* more, were a part of her stance. Her feelings of needing to prove, to earn respect, to do good in order to be good emerged at every turn; very much like Saul before the Damascus Road. She wanted to start a preschool for the economically deprived. She would like to work in a tutoring program in the Mexican-American community. What were we doing about family planning in our Mexico mission? Were we really aware of the plight of the elderly?

As inspiring as her dedication to humanity was, I always felt a bit depressed after being with her. Though we shared a common commitment, and she began to reveal some hidden corners of her inner self, I never felt we made significant personal contact. When our eyes met, it would be only momentarily; she couldn't really look at me. Her slumped body and clenched hands continued to symbolize an uncertain, timid, searching, cowering person.

But this day was different. She had tried to see me a number of times that week, but she hadn't made it. I knew she had made an application to spend six months as a mission volunteer in Latin America, at her own expense. I thought this was what she wanted to talk about. But I was wrong, and when I saw her, I knew it. She was standing straight. She entered my office with a kind of bounce, sat down in a relaxed position, looked at me smilingly, and began to talk.

Who is this? I thought to myself. Certainly not the timid, struggling, frustrated do-gooder I had known three months ago. It was only moments before she was telling a simple but profound story. All the ingredients of self-effortful salvation had been there:

. . . trying to do good so God would accept her;

. . . never feeling "holy enough" or "righteous enough";

. . . laboring in her humanitarian concerns so she could feel comfortable when she prayed;

. . . straining efforts to make everything right in her life in order to sense some worthiness;

the whole scheme of works-righteousness—and all a big dead end! Then she learned that God loved her just as she was. How she learned it is another story, but she learned it—that God loved her and accepted her as she was. She didn't earn that love, nor could she. She couldn't buy it, or ever deserve it. Yet, she was loved and accepted.

Somehow that fact got through to her and changed her life. She used a marvelous symbol to explain her experience, "I was trying to pry open the window to get in the house when all the time the door was open, and I had only to walk in" (*AC*, pp. 15–17).

Janet is different now, changed, free, confident, filled with meaning, alive. In Christian language, we call her experience justification by grace through faith.

Reflecting and Recording

Look back over your Christian journey. Is there any similarity to Janet's? Spend a few minutes reflecting on your journey against the backdrop of Janet's story.

During the Day

Memory is a precious gift of God. We don't use our memory enough. Memorizing is a powerful tool for spiritual growth. We will seek to use that tool during these seven weeks of intentional growth.

Let's begin now. Memorize Phillips translation of Colossians 1:27: "The secret is simply this: Christ *in you!*" Yes, Christ *in you* bringing with him the hope of all the glorious things to come."

Decide now that at your coffee break today (or some time in midmorning), as you sit down to eat lunch, in midafternoon, and before dinner, you will pause, repeat that verse to yourself (aloud if you are in a place where that is possible), and reflect a moment on the fantastic possibility the verse suggests.

Day Two: *Jesus Placarded upon His Cross*

We ourselves are Jews by birth, not Gentiles and sinners. But we know that no man is ever justified by doing what the law demands, but only through faith in Christ Jesus; so we too have put our faith in Jesus Christ, in order that we might be justified through this faith, and not through deeds dictated by law; for by such deeds, Scripture says, no mortal man shall be justified.

If now, in seeking to be justified in Christ, we ourselves no less than the Gentiles turn out to be sinners against the law, does that mean that Christ is an abettor of sin? No, never! No, if I start building up again a system which I have pulled down, then it is that I show myself up as a transgressor of the law. For through the law I died to law—to live for God. I have been crucified with Christ: the life I now live is not my life, but the life which Christ lives in me; and my present bodily life is lived by faith in the Son of God, who loved me and gave himself up for me. I will not nullify the grace of God; if righteousness comes by law, then Christ died for nothing.

—Galatians 2:15–21, NEB

Paul's most reasoned presentation of justification by grace through faith is in his Letter to the Romans. That letter is carefully thought out, deliberately and systematically stated, meditatively reasoned. His Letter to the Galatians is more an outpouring of his thoughts from the top of his head and his feelings from the bottom of his heart. It is in this Letter to the Galatians that he gives his most vivid description of his own life in Christ. In Galatians 2:20 he says, "I have been crucified with Christ; it is no longer I who live, but Christ who lives in me; and the life I now live in the flesh I live by faith in the Son of God, who loved me and gave himself for me." This testimony follows Paul's immortal expression of the heart of the gospel in Galatians 2:16: "A man is not justified by works of the law but through faith in Jesus Christ."

When Paul talks about Jesus he is talking about the entire Christ event—all Christ was and did. For him the message was clear. He had experienced it on the Damascus Road, and the meaning of it was deepened as he reflected and prayed in the Arabian desert before he began to preach that message to any who would listen: Jesus Christ, crucified and risen—and all *for us*. The whole New Testament is completely sure of one thing: all that Jesus Christ did in his life and death was, in the words of the creed, "for us men and for our salvation."

Paul couldn't understand how the Galatians could spurn this message. He was boiling with consternation and stormed at them as the third chapter of his letter begins: "O senseless Galatians, who has put the evil eye on you—you before whose very eyes Jesus Christ was placarded upon His Cross?" (Gal. 3:1 Barclay).

Fire was in Paul's heart and in his pen. To capture the burning intensity of this address, Phillips translated it, "O you dear idiots of Galatia...who has been casting a spell over you?" The New English Bible has it, "You stupid Galatians! You must have been bewitched." How could you miss it—"you before whose eyes Jesus Christ was openly displayed upon his cross"? (*AC,* pp. 20–21).

The way William Barclay translated Galatians 3:1 ("you before whose very eyes Jesus Christ was placarded upon His Cross") is enhanced when you know that the Greek word *prographein* which he rendered *placarded* was a word used for putting up a poster. It meant post a notice as on a bulletin board in a public square. It was also a word Paul used for preaching. In New Testament times, the word was used for what a father did to publicly proclaim that he would bear no responsibility for his son's debts.

Jesus Christ, *placarded* on his cross, proclaims just the opposite. The message posted on the bulletin board of our hearts is that, through the crucified Christ, the Father has taken responsibility for our debts. Our sin-debts are paid. Faith in what God has done in Jesus Christ is what justifies us.

Reflecting and Recording

Yesterday you were asked to look back over your Christian journey in a very general way. Today be more specific. Below is a time line for your life. Beginning at the left designate whatever time in your life you began to be conscious of religious questions, yearnings, growth, struggle. Let the right end of the line designate the present. Move through your life and designate specific experiences or periods of time when you were keenly aware of something of a spiritual nature taking place. Occasions such as baptism, confirmation, conversion, vocational decisions, particular commitments, church involvements may be pegs upon which to hang your reflections. Number these in sequence on the time line (1, 2, 3, etc).

Spiritual Growth Begins   *Present*

_____

Now write a brief word about each of these experiences or period of time in the numbered spaces. (If more than five, use the added space.)

1.

2.

3.

4.

5.

Could any single one of these experiences be described as your ''justification by grace through faith'' experience? Think about it.

* * *

(Remember, when you come to these symbols, please stop; do not read any further—think and reflect as you are requested to do in order to internalize the ideas being shared or the experience reflected upon.)

If there is not a single experience on your time line, how would you explain or interpret that fact in your life?

* * *

During the Day

Janet's story (which we shared yesterday) pictured a person struggling to be accepted by God, to be Christian. As you move through this day and the days ahead, examine your motives for doing what you do. See if your motives tell you anything about whether you actually believe you are justified by grace through faith.

Day Three: *Abiding in Christ*

For two years, 1980 and 1981, I lived with Paul's Letters to the Galatians, Ephesians, Philippians, Colossians, and Philemon. I wrote a commentary on these letters published as Volume 8 in *The Communicator's Commentary* (Word Books, Waco, Texas, 1982).

Even before I began this study, my life and study of prayer had convinced me that the *experience of the indwelling Christ* is the heart and nerve of our Christian pilgrimage. Immersing myself in these five epistles, I have become convinced, with Dr. James Stewart, that this concept is the key which unlocks the secrets of Paul's soul.

Within the Holy of Holies which stood revealed when the veil was rent in twain from the top to the bottom on the day of Damascus, Paul beheld Christ summoning and welcoming him in infinite love into vital unity with Himself. If one seeks for the most characteristic sentences the apostle ever wrote, they will be found, not where he is refuting the legalists, or vindicating his apostleship, or meditating on eschatological hopes, or giving practical ethical guidance to the Church, but where his intense intimacy with Christ comes to expression. Everything that religion meant for Paul is focused for us in such great words as these: "I live, yet not I, but Christ liveth in me" [Gal. 2:20]. "There is, therefore, now no condemnation to them which are in Christ Jesus" [Rom. 8:1] "He that is joined unto the Lord is one spirit." [I Cor. 6:17] (Stewart, p. 147).

It is interesting that Paul does not tell about his Damascus Road experience in descriptive detail. Luke records that dramatic event in the Acts of the Apostles. Paul doesn't recount an outward description of the experience—being struck down by a blinding light and hearing the voice of Christ. Rather, he talks about the *meaning* of that experience and almost sings about it in exulting joy: "I have been crucified with Christ; it is no longer I who live, but Christ who lives in me; and the life I now live in the flesh I live by faith in the Son of God, who loved me and gave himself for me" (Gal. 2:20, RSV).

Paul's two great concepts—justification by grace through faith and Christ indwelling us—are brought together in this one-line biography.

That was Paul. Look now at Jesus. In his challenging image of the vine and the branches, he tells us who he is in relation to God, and who we are in relation to him.

I am the real vine; my Father is the vinedresser. He removes any of my branches which are not bearing fruit and he prunes every branch that does bear fruit to increase its yield. Now, you have already been pruned by my words. You must go on growing in me and I will grow in you. For just as the branch cannot bear any fruit unless it shares the life of the vine, so you can produce nothing unless you go on growing in me. I am the vine itself; you are the branches. It is the man who shares my life and whose life I share who proves fruitful. For the plain fact is that apart from me you can do nothing at all.

—John 15:1–5, PHILLIPS

Extravagant—but reality! Simple, but not simplistic! Jesus came for one purpose and one purpose alone—to bring himself to us and in bringing himself to bring God. Not only does he justify us by providing full *pardon* for our sin, he indwells us to give us the *power* to be and do all those things God requires us to be and do. The message of justification by faith is our evangelistic proclamation which must never be diminished. It is crucial. However, it is not complete.

We talk about becoming Christian in ways like "accepting Christ," "inviting Christ into our lives," "receiving Christ as Savior," "being born again by allowing Christ to be born in us." Whatever the language, the faith and experience is that as we confess and repent of our sins, we are forgiven. We are justified, accepted by, and enter into a new relationship with God who then lives in us through the power of his Spirit as the indwelling Christ (*AC*, p. 25).

Reflecting and Recording

The astonishing fact is that Christians are to be alive in Christ. This reality follows: The presence of God in Jesus Christ is to be experienced not only on occasion, but the indwelling Christ is to become the shaping power of our lives. Ponder this reality and write your response here. In your reflection, ask questions like these: Is this new "news" for me? Have I heard it before? Where? If not, why not? Am I living as though it were true? What in my life reflects this reality of the shaping power of the indwelling Christ? Make notes here and on the next page.

During the Day

On Day One you memorized Colossians 1:27: "The secret is simply this: Christ *in you!*" Now memorize this truth: *The presence of God in Jesus Christ is to be experienced not only on occasion, but the indwelling Christ is to become the shaping power of my life*. Take that powerful reality with you, along with Paul's word, and call them to mind as often as possible.

Day Four: *A Definition: Spiritual Formation*

Spiritual formation is that dynamic process of receiving through faith and appropriating through commitment, discipline, and action, the living Christ into our own life to the end that our life will conform to and manifest the reality of Christ's presence in the world.

This definition is a mind-full. Go back and read it again.

✳   ✳   ✳

Some years ago I met a man through the mail—a Trappist monk who was then eighty-two. We have corresponded a lot and his letters sparkle with life. Though I have spent only one day with him in his monastery in Oregon, I count him among my precious friends.

We spent much of our time the day we were together talking about *the indwelling Christ* and the *real presence* of Christ in Holy Communion. A few months later I shared in a moving worship experience with Roman Catholics but was denied the bread and wine in the celebration of Holy Communion. When, in a letter to Brother Simon, I expressed my pain at not being given the opportunity of sharing fully in this sacrament of life and joy, by return mail I received this reply:

"My dear Brother Maxie:

"I made contact this week with the very soul of you, early in the week, by mental telepathy and by letter. Wednesday and Thursday, my supraconscious started registering 'Maxie, Maxie, Maxie' by its spiritual morse dot-and-dash code. That set me Hail-Marying for the Dunnams and made me tack Jerry's [my wife] 'Fresh Every Morning' poster below my daily calendar, to the left of my room door. So, it is Dunnams my coming in and Dunnams my going out.

"I asked Lady Guadalupe [the patron saint of their monastery] how to tell Maxie about Jesus in the Blessed Sacrament. She said use Jerry and the word 'ontological.' So, He's there ontologically. Body and Blood, Soul and Divinity, whether I think of him now and then or don't. Why Jerry? Kim [our oldest daughter] was with her one month, ontologically before either she, Jerry, or you knew it—a living existence, independent of your thought of it—there and how God willed her to be there. As a boy in church, I remember saying, 'I wish I lived when Jesus did live.' The answer came immediately, 'You are living with me now, I am living here with you.' He's been living with me ever since. Sort of first-month Kim-like. I confess, occasionally I have tried to dodge His presence. But then my whole world crashed, and I hurried back to his energizing, chastened and secure. Therefore, I can feel your pain in not communing completely. Jesus loved His disciples. How He hurt when they left Him, when they heard His hard words, 'My Body, My Blood.' The loneliest words ever uttered were those He addressed to the Apostles putting them 'on their own.' 'Will you leave me?' I never tire loving Peter for keeping Him company in that moment of His agony of not being wanted, God though He was, though so hidden a one by free choice.

"I've been reading things about teaching children math. One teacher told her pupil, 'Use your imagination when I ask you, if you have 9 goodies in your right hand and 7 in your left, how many have you?' Pupil, 'Fourteen.' Teacher, 'Wrong, 7 and 9 are 16.' 'I know that,' the pupil answered, 'but you said use your imagination, so I ate one, gave one away, so 14 is the correct answer!' *Is faith using imagination in this sense?*

"Your Maxie image in a mirror has no Maxie substance, but it is Maxie nonetheless."

mind-boggling, unbelievable, extravagant, radical—with what word would you respond to this heart-stopping possibility? That we "may attain to fullness of being, the fullness of God himself"! Earlier in his epistle Paul talked about the "fullness of God" being fully present in Christ and that fullness permeating the Church which is Christ's body (Eph. 1:10-23). He had hinted at, and now he makes bold the fact that this promise is a possibility for every person: *that we may be filled with all the fullness of God.*

Paul is clear about how we attain this "fullness of being."

God, rich in mercy,...brought us to life with Christ even when we were dead in our sins....And in union with Christ Jesus he raised us up...so that we might display in the ages to come how immense are the resources of his grace, and how great his kindness to us in Christ Jesus....We are God's handiwork, created in Christ Jesus to devote ourselves to the good deeds for which God has designed us. (Eph. 2:4–10 NEB)

"In Christ," "In union with Christ," "Christ dwelling in our hearts"—these recurring phrases capture Paul's conviction of the good news. "Fullness of being, the fullness of God himself," is ours through Christ who indwells us. It is in this reality of the indwelling Christ that my understanding of spiritual formation is rooted. It is in this reality of the indwelling Christ that prayer as a specific act and prayerful living, for me, has taken on fresh, vibrant, and powerful meaning (*AC*, pp. 41–42).

Reflecting and Recording

Go back and read Ephesians 3:14–19 printed on page 27.

✳   ✳   ✳

The climax and summary of that passage is the last sentence: "So may you attain to fullness of being, the fullness of God himself." Now think on this: The goal of Christian prayer and spiritual formation is for us to be filled with all the fullness of God.

In three or four sentences, write your response to this claim—do you believe it? Is it happening in your life? How might it happen? Would you like it to happen?

During the Day

On Day One I shared my morning ritual—the word I speak to myself: "[Maxie,] the secret is simply this: Christ *in you*! Yes, Christ *in you* bringing with him the hope of all the glorious things to come." I asked you to memorize and use it that day. Now I'd like to urge you to make that your daily ritual. On awakening each morning, call your name and speak the word to yourself: "_____, the secret is simply this . . ."

Day Six: *A Clarifying Word*

The word *union* is a common one in spirituality. We talk about being in union with God. A central concept in some religions is *oneness*. The individual becomes nothing, loses self in universal spirit, is merged into the flow of the eternal. This is not Christian spirituality.

Christian spirituality recognizes that union with God does not abolish the separate identities of the Divine and human. In union with God, or in Paul's word, being filled with all the fullness of God, our individuality is enhanced, and we become fully the unique persons God created us to be.

Jan van Ruysbroek compared the relationship between God and humankind to an iron and fire.

> That measureless love which is God himself dwells in the pure deeps of our spirit, like a burning brazier of coals. And it throws forth brilliant and fiery sparks which stir and enkindle heart and senses, will and desire, and all the powers of the soul, with a fire of love. . . . As air is penetrated by the brightness and heat of the sun, and iron is penetrated by fire, so that it works through fire the works of fire, since it burns and shines like the fire . . . yet each of these keeps its own nature—the fire does not become iron, and the iron does not become fire. So likewise is God in the being of the soul . . . The creature never becomes God, nor does God ever become the creature.

So how are we in union with Christ? By the power of the Holy Spirit present as the indwelling Christ. This concept lends itself to confusion also, thus another clarifying word.

In the great comfort chapter, John 14, Jesus says: "I will not leave you desolate; I will come to you . . . and he who loves me will be loved by my Father, and I will love him and manifest myself to him." (18–21, RSV). He then explains in verses 23–28 how he will dwell with the disciples, making it clear that his Spirit, the Spirit of God, will be an abiding presence and the source of life.

> If a man loves me, he will keep my word, and my Father will love him, and we will come to him and make our home with him. He who does not love me does not keep my words; and the word which you hear is not mine but the Father's who sent me.
>
> These things I have spoken to you, while I am still with you. But the Counselor, the Holy Spirit, whom the Father will send in my name, he will teach you all things, and bring to your remembrance all that I have said to you. Peace I leave with you; my peace I give to you; not as the world gives do I give to you. Let not your hearts be troubled, neither let them be afraid. You heard me say to you, "I go away, and I will come to you." If you loved me, you would have rejoiced, because I go to the Father; for the Father is greater than I. And now I have told you before it takes place, so that when it does take place, you may believe. I will no longer talk much with you, for the ruler of this world is coming. He has no power over me; but I do as the Father has commanded me, so that the world may know that I love the Father. Rise, let us go hence.

—John 14:23–31, RSV

Throughout the writings of John and of Paul, the Holy Spirit, the Spirit of God, and the Spirit of Christ are indistinguishable and are used interchangeably.

In chapter 15 of John, following Jesus' promise of the Counselor in chapter 14, Jesus gives that marvelous picture of the vine and branches at which we looked on Day Three. This image provided the foundation for Jesus' followers, especially Paul, to understand the Spirit of Christ being with us and we in him. A classic expression of this is Romans 8: 9–11:

> But that is not how you live. You are on the spiritual level, if only God's Spirit dwells within you; and if a man does not possess the Spirit of Christ, he is no Christian. But if Christ is dwelling within you, then although the body is a dead thing because you sinned, yet the spirit is life itself because you have been justified. Moreover, if the Spirit of him who raised Jesus from the dead dwells within you, then the God who raised Christ Jesus from the dead will also give new life to your mortal bodies through his indwelling Spirit.
> —Romans 8:9–11, NEB

Can you see in this passage any distinction between Christ dwelling within us and the Holy Spirit? I can't. So we restate our earlier affirmation: We are in union with Christ by the power of the Holy Spirit present as the indwelling Christ.

Reflecting and Recording

We learn and truth comes alive experientially by repetition—by affirming and reaffirming truth as we perceive it. So keep doing it. Pause for a while after each affirmation and let it sink in.

The presence of God in Jesus Christ is to be experienced not only on occasion, but the indwelling Christ is to become the shaping power of our lives.

✳   ✳   ✳

I have been crucified with Christ; it is no longer I who lives, but Christ who lives in me; and the life I now live in the flesh I live by faith in the Son of God, who loved me and gave himself for me (Gal. 2:20, RSV).

✳   ✳   ✳

(_____), the secret is simply this: Christ *in you*! Yes, Christ *in you* bringing with him the hope of all the glorious things to come (Col. 1:27, PHILLIPS).

During the Day

Yesterday we defined *prayerful living* as recognizing, cultivating awareness of, and giving expression to the indwelling Christ.

List three or four ways you will do that during this and the coming days:

1.

2.

3.

4.

Be very specific and look forward to your next waking day. Which of these ways of prayerful living will you put into practice? Commit yourself now to do it.

Day Seven: *God Lives in Us through the Power of God's Spirit as the Indwelling Christ*

Next week we will focus on dying and rising with Christ as the metaphor for our life in Christ. We close this week by continuing our central thought of yesterday which is in this succinct statement: *God lives in us through the power of God's Spirit as the indwelling Christ.*

Albert Outler, distinguished theologian and perceptive observer and interpreter of church history, contends that we are on the verge of a third great awakening. Above all, he says this awakening will be "an unprogrammed outpouring of the Holy Spirit." I personally believe the outpouring has begun and the "charismatic renewal" is witness to this.

This current emphasis on the Holy Spirit is confusing to many and in many instances divisive in churches. The reason for the confusion may be that the church has given too little attention to the Holy Spirit. So the response of many in our churches to this emphasis is that of the people when Paul asked, "Did you receive the Holy Spirit when you believed? . . . We have never even heard that there is a Holy Spirit," his hearers responded (Acts 19:2).

Another source of confusion, and certainly the cause of divisiveness, is dogmatism. Too many within what is popularly called "charismatic renewal" or the "Holy Spirit Movement" are too dogmatic, too intent on a system of rigid experience, the ultimate of which is labeled "the baptism of the Holy Spirit." Unfortunately, many insist that you do not have "the baptism" unless certain signs such as speaking in tongues are present.

One thing is clear from the New Testament: there is no awareness of the presence of the Risen Christ to us or in us except through the Holy Spirit, and there can be no convincing validation of the claim that one has the Holy Spirit unless this is accompanied by signs of Jesus' presence, the chief sign of which is love.

You may say it either way. The Holy Spirit is present in us as the indwelling Christ or Christ is present in us as the Holy Spirit. This is the reason Schleiermacher could say, "The fruits of the Spirit are nothing but the virtues of Christ." (*AC*, pp. 47–48).

As we grow in being alive in Christ, every part of our life is connected with Christ. The process of spiritual formation is the process of learning to say yes to Christ every day in every way. Later on in our journey we will give specific attention to the indwelling Christ as a converting presence. I doubt if there will come a time in any of our lives when we will not need to change; when some aspect of our being, newly discovered, will not need the transforming power of Christ brought to bear upon it. I doubt if the time will ever come—though I pray for it for myself—when we can say with all confidence and certainly, "I'm yours, Lord. Everything about me, and of me, is yours." For even as we pray that prayer, revelation comes, and a hidden area or concern emerges to awareness, and we have to make another commitment, and yield ourselves to transforming love.

And that's what it is all about. Spiritual formation is that dynamic process of receiving through faith and appropriating through commitment, discipline, and action, the living Christ into our own life to the end that our life will conform to, and manifest the reality of, Christ's presence in the world.

Reflecting and Recording

Go back to Day One and flip slowly through the pages, noting what you may have underlined, reflecting briefly on what you have written in your recording spaces, and get a kind of running "feel" of this week's work. Sense movement, the great scriptural affirmations and bold statements of faith—and yourself at the center of it all. Sit quietly and pray as you are led about this exciting journey to aliveness in Christ.

During the Day

If you are a part of a group sharing this workbook, you will probably be meeting sometime today or tonight. Read the instructions for that meeting and prepare to share. Your sharing will contribute to God's intention for the group. Don't withold your gifts.

If you are not a part of a group, during this day find someone with whom to share personally some of the insights and challenges that have come to you from your workbook so far.

Group Meeting for Week One

Introduction

These group sessions will be most meaningful as they reflect the experience of all the participants. This guide is simply an effort to facilitate personal sharing. Therefore, do not be rigid in following these suggestions. The leader, especially, should seek to be sensitive to what is going on in the lives of the participants and to focus the group sharing on those experiences. Ideas are important. We should wrestle with new ideas as well as with ideas with which we disagree. It is important, however, that the group meeting not become a debate about ideas. The emphasis should be on persons—experiences, feelings, and meaning.

As the group comes to the place where all can share honestly and openly what is happening in their lives, the more meaningful the experience will be. This does not mean sharing only the good or positive; share also the struggles, the difficulties, the negatives.

Discipline is not easy; it is deceptive to pretend it is. Growth requires effort. Don't be afraid to share your questions, reservations, and "dry periods," as well as that in which you find meaning.

Sharing Together

1. You may begin your time together by allowing time for each person in the group to share his or her most meaningful day with the workbook this week. The leader should begin this sharing. Tell why that particular day was so meaningful.

2. Now share your most difficult day. Tell what you experienced and why it was so difficult.

3. On Day Two, you were asked to plot your Christian journey and to write briefly about some of these experiences. Ask all persons who will to share what they may see as their "justification by grace through faith" experience or their struggle to feel accepted by God, to be Christian.

Praying Together.

Each week the group is asked to pray together. Corporate prayer is one of the great blessings of Christian community. There is power in corporate prayer, and it is important that this dimension be included in our shared pilgrimage.

It is also important that you feel comfortable in this and that no pressure be placed on anyone to pray aloud. *Silent* corporate prayer may be as vital and meaningful as verbal corporate prayer.

God does not need to hear our verbal words to hear our prayers. Silence, where thinking is centered and attention is focused, may provide our deepest periods of prayer. There is power, however, in a community on a common journey verbalizing their thoughts and feelings to God in the presence of their fellow pilgrims.

Verbal prayers should be offered spontaneously as a person chooses to pray aloud—not "let's go around the circle now, and each one pray."

Suggestions for this "praying together" time will be given each week. The leader for the week should regard these only as suggestions. What is happening in the meeting—the mood, the needs that are expressed, the timing—should determine the direction of the group praying together. Here are some possibilities for this closing period.

1. Let the group think back over the sharing that has taken place during this session. What personal needs or concerns came out of the sharing? Begin to speak these aloud—any person verbalizing a need or a concern that has been expressed. Don't hesitate to mention a concern that you may have picked up from another, i.e., "Mary isn't able to be with us this week because her son is in the hospital. Let's pray for her son and for her."

It will be helpful for each person to make notes of the concerns and needs that are mentioned. Enter deliberately into a period of silence. Let the leader verbalize each of these needs successively, allowing for a brief period following each so that persons in the group may center their attention and focus their prayers on the person, need, or concern mentioned. All of this will be in silence as each person prays in *his* or *her own way*.

2. Let the leader close this time of sharing and silent prayer by asking the group to share in a prayer liturgy. The leader will call the name of each person in the group, after which the group will say, "Lord, bless him/her" as they focus their eyes on that person. Let the person whose name is called look at each person in the room to catch their eye and receive their ''look'' of blessing as well as their word. When this is done, the leader calls the next name, until all are ''blessed'' and looked at with a blessing. Then the leader may simply say, ''Amen.''

Picture Taking: If someone has an instant camera (polaroid) take a picture of each person in group. Turn pictures face down on table and let each person take one. This is the person for whom you will pray specifically this week. Before you go, take a few minutes to visit with the person whose picture you chose, getting to know him/her better. Ask if there are things coming up in that person's life about which you might pray.

Dying and Rising with Christ

Day One: *Buried with Christ*

See to it that no one makes a prey of you by philosophy and empty deceit, according to human tradition, according to the elemental spirits of the universe, and not according to Christ. For in him the whole fulness of deity dwells bodily, and you have come to fulness of life in him, who is the head of all rule and authority. In him also you were circumcised with a circumcision made without hands, by putting off the body of flesh in the circumcision of Christ; and you were buried with him in baptism, in which you were also raised with him through faith in the working of God, who raised him from the dead. And you, who were dead in trespasses and the uncircumcision of your flesh, God made alive together with him, having forgiven us all our trespasses, having canceled the bond which stood against us with its legal demands; this he set aside, nailing it to the cross. He disarmed the principalities and powers and made a public example of them, triumphing over them in him.''

—Colossians 2:8–15, RSV

I have a friend who is a Benedictine monk. The way we live out our lives is vastly different, but I feel a real kinship, a oneness of spirit with Brother Sam. One of the most meaningful memories, to which I return often in my mind, is an evening he and I spent together alone, sharing our Christian journeys. The vivid highlight of that evening, still alive in my mind, was his sharing with me the occasion of his solemn vows, the service when he made his life commitment to the Benedictine community and the monastic life.

On that occasion he prostrated himself before the altar of the chapel in the very spot where his coffin will be set when he dies. Covered in a funeral pall, the death bell that tolls at the earthly parting of a brother sounded the solemn gongs of death. Then there was silence—the silence of death. THe silence of the gathered community was broken by the singing of the Colossian word: "For you have died, and your life is hid with Christ in God" (Col. 3:3). After that powerful word, there was more silence as Brother Sam reflected on his solemn vow. Then the community broke into song with the words of Psalm 118, which is always a part of the Easter liturgy in the Benedictine community: "I shall not die, but live, and declare the works of the Lord" (Ps. 118:17 KJV).

After this resurrection proclamation, the deacon shouted the word from Ephesians: "Awake, O sleeper, and arise from the dead, and Christ will give you light" (Eph. 5:14). Then the bells of the Abbey rang loudly and joyfully, Brother Sam rose, the funeral pall fell off, and the robe of the Benedictine order was placed on him. He received the kiss of peace and was welcomed into the community to live a life "hid in Christ."

This great liturgy of death and resurrection is a symbolic reenactment of the Christian experience. When I heard it I relived my baptism in a cold creek in September in rural Mississippi. Paul gave powerful witness to this experience over and over again: I have been crucified with Christ; I am now alive in him (*AC*, pp. 27–28).

Being buried with Christ is the language of baptism. More important, it is the fact of baptism—dying and rising—and the heart of the Christian life. A few years ago I saw the "death door" of St. Peter's in Rome. It depicts a series of death scenes: Death by falling, death by war, the martyr death of Peter upside down on a cross. Death by water was also there, and I reasoned this was behind the sculptor's theme. We enter the faith by death. Baptism, our acted out entrance into the church, is by water. So, water baptism is symbolic of death. The early church often built its baptismal fonts in the shape of tombs to make the meaning graphic.

Reflecting and Recording

In the days ahead we will continue our reflection on this symbol of being buried with Christ. For now, reflect on your own Christian experience as you hold in your mind the image of being buried with Christ and remember the experience of Brother Sam. Have you had a parallel experience—maybe not as dramatic, but one that marked a designated entry into the Christian faith, and/or the church? Relive such an experience by describing it in writing here.

During the Day

Are you practicing the morning ritual—''(   ), the secret is simply this . . .''? If not, I hope you will give it a try. If so, continue it.

During this particular day, carry with you the memory of the experience you described above. Let it invigorate you by giving you confidence in who you are.

Day Two: *Nobodies Become Somebodies*

In his book, *The Gospel for the Person Who Has Everything*, Will

Willimon tells about a young friend, age four, who was asked on the occasion of his fifth birthday what kind of party he wanted to have.

"I want everyone to be a king or a queen," Clayton said.

"So, he and his mother went to work fashioning a score of silver crowns (cardboard and aluminum foil), purple robes (crepe paper), and royal scepters (a stick painted gold). On the day of the party, as the guests arrived, they were each given their royal crown, robe, and scepter and were thus dressed as a king or a queen. It was a regal sight—all kings and queens. Everyone had a wonderful time. They all ate ice cream and cake. Then they had a procession up to the end of the block and back again. All in all, it was a royal, wonderful day.

That evening, as Clayton's mom was tucking him into bed, she asked him what he wished when he blew the candles out on his birthday cake.

"I wished," he said, "that *everyone* in the whole world could be a king or a queen—not just on my birthday, but *every* day" (Willimon, pp. 30–31).

My friend, Will, closed that story by saying, "Well, Clayton, baptism shows that something very much like that happened one day at a place called Calvary. We who were nobodies became somebodies. Those who were no people became God's people. The wretched of the earth became royalty."

Isn't that a marvelous image? Baptism is symbolic of our passing from death to life through Jesus Christ. It is the sacrament of the church that marks the claiming of our true identity, the fact that we have been named by God as God's people through the church—that we *nobodies* have become *somebodies*. Peter put it this way in his epistle: "Once you were no people, but now you are God's people; once you had not received mercy but now you have received mercy" (1 Peter 2:10, RSV).

Again, Will Willimon reminds us that:

in the earliest baptismal liturgies, after the person had been baptized, he or she appeared before the bishop who embraced the new Christian and then did something of great significance: The bishop dipped his finger into oil and made the sign of the cross on the new Christian's forehead. This was known as the *signation*. The sign of the cross upon a person's forehead was like a brand to show ownership. As sheep are marked to show ownership, so Christians are marked, by baptism, to show who owns them and to what flock they belong. Christians are branded to show who chose them and who owns them. (Willimon, p. 41).

Reflecting and Recording

I want to propose two lines of reflection today.

For those who have been baptized. Reflect on your baptism. What sort of meaning has it had for you? If baptized as an infant, reflect on what you have been taught—how you have claimed that experience, either in confirmation, or in an adult, public profession of faith. Just what does baptism mean to you? Write your reflections here.

For those who have not been baptized. Have you had some experience comparable in your mind to baptism? Why have you not been baptized? Have you considered it? What meaning do you attach to baptism? Write your reflections here.

During the Day

A few years ago, a young minister made and gave me a beautiful plaque. On it is a lovely seashell my friend found on the beach (the shell is symbolic of baptism), and the words: REMEMBER YOUR BAPTISM.

That plaque is on the right doorpost of our exit from the kitchen—the door we use most frequently when leaving home. So every day, sometimes numerous times, that challenging word greets me as I leave home. REMEMBER YOUR BAPTISM. During the day, as I stay alive to the fact of my baptism, it influences my relationships, my attitudes, and my actions.

Take that thought with you today. Even if you have not been baptized, you have been claimed by God. So at all times during the day—approaching a tough task, wrestling with a crucial decision, working in a difficult relationship—announce to yourself: "I have been baptized. I have been claimed by God."

Day Three: *Hidden with Christ in God*

Since, then, you have been raised with Christ, set your heart on things above, where Christ is seated at the right hand of God. Set your minds on things above, not on earthly things. For you died, and your life is now hidden with Christ in God. When Christ, who is your life appears, then you also will appear with him in glory.

—Colossians 3:1–4, NIV

To be a Christian is to change. It is to become new. It is not simply a matter of choosing a new life-style, though there is a new style. It has to do with being a new person. The new person does not emerge full grown. Conversion, passing from life to death, may be the miracle of a moment, but the making of a saint is the task of a lifetime. The dynamic process of saint-making is to work out in fact what is already true in principle. In *position,* in our relation to God in Jesus Christ, we are new persons; that is justification. Now our *condition,* the actual life that we live, must be brought into harmony with our new position. That is the process of sanctification.

A man once said to Dwight L. Moody, "Sir, I am a self-made-man." Moody replied, "You have saved the Lord from a very great responsibility." It is the Lord who made us and who remakes us. Two things happened in the fall, and in our own fall. The first is that we became *estranged* from God. Second, [God's] image within us was broken, distorted, defaced. Two things happen in salvation. First, we are *reconciled* to God; our estrangement is dissolved by the justifying grace of God in the cross of Jesus. Our status is changed; we become friends of God. We are no longer strangers separated and at enmity with God; we are accepted by [God] as though we were without sin. Second, there is the re-creation of the image of God in the life of the believer. This is the reason John Wesley talked about grace impinging upon us and working in three specific ways: prevenient grace, justifying grace, sanctifying grace. Prevenient grace is the grace of God going before us, pulling us, wooing us, tenderizing our hearts, seeking to open our minds and hearts, and eventually giving us faith. Even the faith we exercise for our justification is the result of [God's] grace. Justifying faith is our trustful obedient response to Christ—his life, death, and resurrection—as our only means of salvation. Sanctifying grace is the work of Christ within us, his Spirit restoring the broken image, completing what has begun in justification.

It is this restoration work of God's grace to which we have given too little attention. In my church tradition, the Methodist, we have a glaring illustration of failure. In the latter part of the nineteenth century a revival of emphasis on holiness began to move through the church. As is so often the case, people began to preach a particularized experience as the norm. Doctrines were clearly and rigidly defined and this portended conflict and division. A big segment of the church objected strenuously to particular ideas about holiness, and especially rejected a notion of "second-blessing sanctification." At the risk of oversimplification, the doctrine of "second-blessing sanctification" claimed that in a second experience of grace like that operative in conversion or justification, a person might have his or her carnal nature eradicated so that one could live a sinless life. Unfortunately for some the doctrine was "cast in concrete," rigidly and tenaciously presented as the norm for Christian life.

Just as tragic as that failure was the reaction of the many who, failing to be able to harmonize the proclamation about perfection and holiness with experienced reality, threw the baby out with the bath. Rejecting an altogether too narrow definition of sanctification or holiness, and fleeing from an obvious stance of self-righteousness, they went to the opposite extreme and forgot sanctification altogether. For decades little attention has been given to "holiness" within the mainstream United Methodist denomination. I'm calling for a new look at, and a new commitment to sanctification, the possibility of holiness or wholeness, the restoration of God's image with us (*AC*, pp. 28–30).

Look again at our definition of spiritual formation: *Spiritual formation* is that dynamic process of receiving through faith and appropriating through commitment, discipline, and action, the living Christ into our own life to the end that our life will conform to, and manifest the reality of Christ's presence in the world.

Paul contended that nothing less than a new creature *perfect in Christ* (Col. 1:28, NIV) is the aim of the Christian life.

He used a striking word to describe it—the word that was a part of the liturgy in Brother Sam's monastic vows: "You died, and your life is now hidden with Christ in God" (Col. 3:3, NIV).

Reflecting and Recording

Tomorrow we will examine the meaning of this passage more fully. For a few minutes now, pursue the meaning of this image in your own life by answering in a couple of sentences the following questions:

1. What does *sanctification* mean to you?

2. What does it mean to die with Christ?

During the Day

This is our paramount image for the day: "hidden with Christ in God." That means God is with you, personally and intimately with you. It means that you are *protected* by God. It means that as you recognize God with you, you are *guided*. It means that a *power* not your own is available, and a *love* not your own surrounds you. Live this day with that image constantly in your mind: *hidden with Christ in God*.

Day Four: *Dead in Christ*

> If we have been united with [Christ] in a death like his, we shall certainly be united with him in a resurrection like his. We know that our old self was crucified with him so that the sinful body might be destroyed, and we might no longer be enslaved to sin. For he who has died is freed from sin. But if we have died with Christ, we believe that we shall also live with him. For we know that Christ being raised from the dead will never die again; death no longer has dominion over him. The death he died he died to sin, once for all, but the life he lives he lives to God. So you also must consider yourselves dead to sin and alive to God in Christ Jesus.
>
> —Romans 6:5–11, RSV.

The Christian is a new person united with Christ. Death and resurrection were the two momentous events through which Jesus passed, and which must be reproduced in the spiritual histories of each Christian. To be *in* and *with* Christ is to be identified with him in death and resurrection. These two events in Jesus' history, and ours, are rivetted together in meaning though we may talk about them separately.

Being crucified with Christ was an experiential fact for Paul, and must be for any Christian. Two words, *pardon* and *power,* capture the big meaning of the death of Christ for us. We tend to emphasize pardon more than power. Certainly there is no question about our need for the pardoning grace of Christ. This was our emphasis last week when we focused on justification by grace through faith.The total and complete forgiveness for past sins must never be minimized. Jesus, in his death on the cross, made dramatically and forever clear the nature of God which he had portrayed so poignantly in the parable of the Prodigal Son. The central lesson of that parable is that when the prodigal son returned home, the father received him as though he had never been away. That's pardon—extravagant grace—unconditional love.

But there is more than pardon in our identification with Jesus' death; there is power.

When Paul talked about the death of Christ and our participation in that death, he was thinking not only of forgiveness for past sins, but of a drastic break with sin, a demolishing of sin's dominion over our lives.

Again, for Paul, it was a matter of death and resurrection. "Consider yourselves dead to sin and alive to God in Christ Jesus" (Rom. 6:11). No longer are we "enslaved to sin" (Rom. 6:6). Our death to sin is final in the same way that Jesus died "once for all." To get the full impact of Paul's magnificent and vigorous claim read chapter 6 of Romans. Realize what has happened, he is saying, a gulf as wide and deep as death is between what you now are and what you once were.

The person whose life is hid with Christ in God is dead to sin because he or she is united with Christ's death which has destroyed the power of sin over us. Christ makes us victors over sin. There is something bold and defiant and jubilant about the way Paul spoke of death to sin and the old life by our sharing in the death of Christ. Faith in Christ means "being made conformable unto his death," having our "nature transformed to die as he died" (Phil. 3:10 Moffatt). The fact is that Christ has destroyed the power of sin. Now, sharing in the death of Christ, we *reckon ourselves dead to sin,* and are empowered to become what we potentially are.

It is difficult to see how persons could get the notion that the sinful aspect of our nature (some refer to this as our carnal nature) could be eradicated or purged. Paul is so bold in his affirmation about our having died with Christ. The perspective we need to keep has also been given us by Paul. After making these bold claims about "reckoning ourselves dead to sin" in Romans 6, he lays bare his own soul in Romans 7, giving us that graphic picture of sin still present in our lives. He says,

I am unspiritual, the purchased slave of sin. I do not even acknowledge my own actions as mine, for what I do is not what I want to do, but what I detest...I know that nothing good lodges in me—in my unspiritual nature, I mean—for though the will to do good is there, the deed is not. The good which I want to do, I fail to do; but what I do is the wrong which is against my will....Miserable creature that I am, who is there to rescue me out of this body doomed to death? (Rom. 7:14b–24 NEB)

A pathetic picture—if it stopped there! But it doesn't. Who will rescue us? God alone, through Jesus Christ our Lord! Thanks be to God! (Rom. 7:25). Even in the midst of sin's continuous presence and pressure in our life, we can be triumphant. So, sharing in Christ's death is no one-time event; it is ongoing. We claim the power of his death over sin daily in order that sin's power will not prevail in our lives. (*AC,* pp. 35–36).

Reflecting and Recording

What do these statements mean to you? Answer in two or three sentences.

1. He is a *victim* of sin.

2. She has won the battle over her sin.

Reflect now on your own experience in relation to the death of Christ. Other than forgiveness and pardon, what meaning does Christ's death have for you?

❊   ❊   ❊

During the Day

Lodge this sentence solidly in your mind. *Participation in Christ's death means not only forgiveness of past sin, but a drastic break with sin, a demolishing of sin's dominion and control over our lives.*

There is no situation you will face today wherein you will need to be a *victim* of sin. It is not inevitable that you *give in* to the temptation to sin. Carry this truth with you, and live this day in the power of the indwelling Christ who conquers sin.

Day Five: *Death Has No Power over Us*

"If we have died with Christ," Paul said, "we *also* live with him" (Rom. 6:8, RSV). This was no isolated claim of Paul, but a central affirmation. Not only do we share in the death of Christ, we share in his resurrection.

The new life into which we enter by conversion is nothing else than the life of Christ himself, Paul insists. He speaks of "the life of Jesus" being "manifested in our bodies" (2 Cor. 4:10, RSV). The "law of the Spirit" which overcomes "the law of sin and death" brings the life which is in Christ Jesus (Rom. 8:2, RSV).

This new life is not different from the old life only in degree; it is a new kind, a new quality of life. Paul makes the radical claim that this new life is nothing less than a new creation (2 Cor. 5:17). Sharing in Christ's resurrection means being raised to newness of life.

This means at least two things—one of which we will look at tomorrow. It means, first, that death has no power over us.

> The risen and exalted Lord conquered death. We do not wait for eternal life; it is ours now. Risen with Christ, the glorious privilege of beginning now the life with Christ which will continue eternally is ours.
>
> Sometimes we tend to discredit thoughts about life after death as mere sentiment. Not so. It is the heart of our faith that God will finish what he has begun, and nothing is finished in this world until God is finished with it. John boldly claims that God will not be finished until he brings into perfect existence "a new heaven and a new earth" (Rev. 21:1). Death has no power over us because in Christ we have begun that new life which transcends death and is being perfected by God. (*AC*, p. 37).

I remember spending the night in a hospital room with my then seventy-six-year old mother. She had had cancer eighteen years before; now it had struck, again. She had had a double mastectomy early that morning. In the middle of the night, she stirred and I awoke. I had the feeling she wanted to talk—to talk about important things, not just to make time-passing conversation.

So, we talked. Life. Death. Family. The future. I hope I never forget one thing she said. "'When you give yourself to the Lord, son, everything has to be all right, no matter what happens."

It was her way of saying she was OK. No matter what happened, she was in the hands of the Lord. She had already died the death that matters.

Reflecting and Recording

Think about your most recent encounter with death. On the lines below, list three or four persons close to that experience of death, members of the family, close friends, persons present at the time of death.

_____

_____

_____

_____

_____

Beside each person's name, make some notes about their responses to death. Do that now.

What do these persons' responses say about the power of death over them? About their faith? Think about that for a few minutes.

✳ ✳ ✳

Now look at your own feelings and responses in relation to the death of someone you deeply loved. Are you confident that, being alive in Christ, death has no power over us? Make some notes about your feelings.

During the Day

How did you do with your ''during the day'' truth of yesterday? Turn back and read that as your suggestion for today.

Day Six: *The Power Which Raised Jesus from the Dead Is Also Our Power*

> I pray that the God of our Lord Jesus Christ, the all-glorious Father, may give you the spiritual powers of wisdom and vision, by which there comes the knowledge of him. I pray that your inward eyes may be illumined, so that you may know what is the hope to which he calls you, what the wealth and glory of the share he offers you among his people in their heritage, and how vast the resources of his power open to us who trust in him.
>
> —Ephesians 1:17–19, NEB

Yesterday we suggested that sharing in Christ's resurrection means at least two things. The first we have already talked about: *Death has no power over us*.

Now the second. Sharing Christ's risen life means that the power which raised Jesus from the dead is also our power. Paul breaks into singing prayer when he thinks of the benefits and privileges belonging to Christians. Read Ephesians 1: 17–19 again.

✳ ✳ ✳

Paul continues his prayer, describing the nature of Christ's power.

It is *resurrection* power—the power God ''exerted in Christ when he raised him from the dead'' (v. 20).

It is *ascension* power—God ''enthroned him at his right hand in the heavenly realms'' (v. 20).

It is *dominion* power—''far above all government and authority, all power and dominion, and . . . put everything in subjection beneath his feet'' (vv. 21–22).

What Paul is saying is that the working power of God in the past can be brought into the present.

This is the paramount miracle—that God's immeasurable power in Christ is available now to redeem us from sin, to energize our wills, to heal the sick, to drive out demons, to renew our spirits, to reconcile our relationships.

Is this our vision of reality? Or, have we reduced the faith to an intellectual conception, a set of dogmas, a religious system to which we give assent and which we practice by rote with no impact in power on our daily lives? The power which raised Jesus from the dead is available to us. There are those who are claiming that power, receiving it for the transformation of their lives (*AC,* p. 38).

I remember being in a city in another state several years ago. I was visiting in a home with a group of people about lunchtime following a Sunday preaching service. I had known the hostess in conferences I had led, but not the host. I'd never met him before. He was a hard-driving business man, the stereotype of success, work above everything; the dream of the good life was the magnet that pulled him on. It was also the situation I see so often: the wife, the religious one; the husband, in church but only body-present for the sake of the family; the wife genuinely seeking a vital spirituality; the husband too busy with other things, too preoccupied with the so-called real world and trapped in the falsehood that spiritual things are not masculine.

For some reason, John and I hit it off that Sunday afternoon. We found ourselves alone out on the balcony of his beautiful home. He talked honestly as I dared to probe a bit and listen. By a miracle of Spirit, soul touched soul. Only a short time before, the huge manufacturing business that he headed had been swallowed up in a conglomerate, and he'd lost his prestigious and powerful position. His world had crumbled, and the ''good life'' that he had finally grasped was fading; it was like sand running out of his fingers, and this towering man was now feeling impotent, no longer in control.

I stayed in touch with John after that first meeting. He wrestled with this lost dream for over a year before he began to get a grip on things and move toward a degree of wholeness. Then something big happened in his life. He attended an Emmaus Walk and had a life-changing experience—life-changing in the sense that it gave him a whole new direction, a whole new approach to life and the resources to deal with it.

This was proven dramatically not long ago. His younger son came ''out of the closet'' and shared the fact that he was a homosexual. I can only imagine how this fellow would have dealt with this shattering experience back when he and I first met. Now, having something new and dynamic going on within him, a Power not his own, he invited his son and wife to sit together and share about this new situation.

The conversation began, "Son, I want you to know there are four persons here—you, your mother and me, and the Holy Spirit. The Holy Spirit is here because I've invited him; I want you to know I love you and I believe the Holy Spirit is going to give us the wisdom and the power to deal with this situation."

What could have been the most destructive estrangement a son and a father could experience had been short-circuited by the power of the Lord, who comes to us as the healing one. Grace, explained only by Christ's presence, is working in a situation that otherwise could have destroyed an entire family. There is a tremendous difference between John when I first met him and John as I know him now.

Reflecting and Recording

Describe an experience in which you participated in the working power of God in the past being brought out of the past into the present. Write enough to really get into the experience in memory again.

Spend a few minutes responding in your mind to this question. Why do I not experience more of what I have just described?

✳   ✳   ✳

During the Day

As you move through the day, remember the barriers that prevent the working power of God in the past being brought into the present—barriers you have thought about as you responded to the question above in reflecting and recording. Try to consciously prevent those barriers from blocking God's power in your life today.

Day Seven: *Dying and Rising with Christ*

We have concentrated our attention this week on Paul's understanding of the Christian life as dying and rising with *Christ*. Let's conclude the week by looking at this central truth as Jesus taught it.

Truly, truly, I say to you, unless a grain of wheat falls into the earth and dies, it remains alone; but if it dies, it bears much fruit. He who loves his life loses it, and he who hates his life in this world will keep it for eternal life. If any one serves me, he must follow me; and where I am, there shall my servant be also; if any one serves me, the Father will honor him.

—John 12:24–26, RSV.

This was not an isolated word of Jesus. He said the same thing in different ways on different occasions. If you are going to find your life, you must lose it. It is only in giving that you receive. If you want to be first, then go to the end of the line. If you are going to be master, take the basin and towel of a servant. All those paradoxes are wrapped in one: We must die if we want to live.

I visited a man recently who was in the hospital, being treated by a psychiatrist for a severe case of depression. It was a sad visit. The man is near retirement, in fact he could retire anytime. Yet he's overcome with fear. He has nothing in store where the future is concerned—or so he thinks and feels. He is paralyzed really, impotent, unable to make decisions.

As we shared together, it became clear that this fellow had never really committed his life to anything—he certainly had never committed his life to Jesus Christ. We talked about that, and the man began to quiver, and his voice grew quiet and shaky as he began to express his reservations. They were more than reservations. He had great fear about what the Lord might require of him if he yielded his life to him.

Here was a man who had come to the verge of retirement lifeless, without meaning on which he could lay hold and without purpose that could propel him into the future. As I left him that day, I remembered the famous evangelist called Christmas Evans. He wore himself out, always on the move, preaching the gospel. His friends kept advising him that he should take things easier. His answer was always, "It is better to burn out than to rust out."

We need to learn from Jesus. *We must die if we want to live:*

In marriage. Marriage that is growing and fulfilling is a dying to-live-process. We die to our own selfish desires in order to meet the needs of our mates.

In all relationships. We can't forever insist on our own way if we are going to value and appreciate others. We die to our own pride of identity in order to live in mutual friendship.

To become Christian. We die to sin and our own efforts to save ourselves, and we come alive to Christ's forgiving grace. To become Christian initially, yes, but also . . .

To become more Christian. We die daily to all that which separates us from God and others, and we come alive to Christ's presence who keeps leading us through death to resurrection.

Dying, we live. We know it, though we find it hard to put into practice. We keep reverting to our old way of seeking to save our lives, so we hoard our resources, protect ourselves, draw back into the security of playing it safe. The way is clear. Jesus marked it: "Unless a grain of wheat falls into the earth and dies, it remains alone; but if it dies, it bears much fruit."

Reflecting and Recording

In the categories listed on the next page, write a few sentences about your need to die in order to live. Be specific. Name ways of relating, habits, attitudes, actions that need to die in order for life to come.

Marriage relationship: _____

_____

_____

_____

Family relationship: _____

_____

_____

_____

Christian life: _____

_____

_____

_____

During the Day

As I suggested last week, if you are a part of a group sharing this workbook, it is important that you share honestly with the other members of this group. That doesn't mean you must share everything you have written or experienced this week. It does mean that *you have something to share and what you share will be helpful to others*. So if you are in a group, read the instructions for the meeting which will probably take place sometime today, and be prepared to enter into that relationship freely and openly.

Whether in a group or not, be sensitive today to those graced moments which will come to give you the opportunity to die in order to live.

Group Meeting for Week Two

Introduction

Participation in a group such as this is a covenant relationship. You will profit most as you keep the daily discipline of the thirty-minute period and as you faithfully attend these weekly meetings. Do not feel guilty if you have to miss a day in the workbook, or be discouraged if you are not able to give the full thirty minutes in daily discipline. Don't hesitate sharing that with the group. We may learn something about ourselves as we share. We may discover, for instance, that we are unconsciously afraid of dealing with the content of a particular day because of what is required and what it reveals about us. Be patient with yourself and always be open to what God my be seeking to teach you.

Our growth, in part, hinges upon our group participation, so share as openly and honestly as you can. Listen to what persons are saying. Sometimes there is meaning beyond the surface of their words which you may pick up if you are really attentive.

Being a sensitive participant in this fashion is crucial. Responding immediately to the feelings we pick up is also crucial. Sometimes it is important for the group to focus its entire attention upon a particular individual. If some need or concern is expressed, it may be appropriate for the leader to ask the group to enter into a brief period of special prayer for the persons or concerns revealed. Participants should not always depend upon the leader for this kind of sensitivity, for the leader may miss it. Even if you aren't the leader, don't hesitate to ask the group to join you in special prayer. This praying may be silent, or some person may wish to lead the group in prayer.

Remember, you have a contribution to make to the group. What you consider trivial or unimportant may be just what another person needs to hear. We are not seeking to be profound but simply to share our experience.

Sharing Together

Note: It will not be possible in this time frame to use all these suggestions. The leader should select what will be most beneficial to the group. It is important that the leader be thoroughly familiar with these suggestions in order to move through them *selectively* according to the direction in which the group is moving and according to the time available. The leader should plan ahead, but do not hesitate to change your plan according to the nature of the sharing taking place and the needs that emerge.

1. Open your time together with the leader offering a brief prayer of thanksgiving for the opportunity of sharing with the group and petitions for openness in sharing and loving response to each other.

2. Let each person share the most meaningful day in this week's workbook adventure.

3. Now share the most difficult day and tell why it was difficult.

4. Dying and rising with Christ and baptism as that acted-out image was the focus of this week. Invite two or three persons to share the experience recorded on Day One in response to Brother Sam's experience of dying and rising with Christ. Each person should take no more than three minutes to share. (*Note*: It is important that persons discipline themselves to use time wisely in sharing. The leader should remind the group of this.)

5. The leader should ask the group, according to the sharing that has taken place thus far, if it would be helpful to spend some time, no more than twelve minutes, talking about what it means to be a victim of and victors over sin. Center on the meaning of this statement: *Participation in Christ's death means not only forgiveness of past sin, but a drastic break with sin, a demolishing of sin's dominion and control over our lives.*

6. Invite anyone who wishes to share an experience verifying the contention that *in Christ* death has no power over us. Time will allow only a couple of persons to share two or three minutes.

7. Dying and rising with Christ means that death no longer has power over us. But it also means the power which raised Jesus from the dead is our power. The working power of God in the past can be brought into the present. (*Note*: This is the crucial issue of this week's focus, so reserve enough time for it.)

On Day Six, we concentrated on this possibility and shared an experience of this fact. Invite three or four persons to take two or three minutes to describe an experience in which they participated in the working power of God being brought into the present. You may want to ask the group to review their "reflecting and recording" on Day Six.

Give the opportunity, after each person shares, for others to respond or ask questions. Questions should not be used to *challenge* but to clarify and enhance meaning.

8. Follow this individual sharing with a discussion of the barriers which prevent us from experiencing more of God's power in our present situation.

9. On Day Seven, our reflecting and recording called for specific response to the dynamic of dying to live in our marriage, our family relationships, and in growing in our Christian life. Invite one person to share in each of these categories. Encourage those who may not have shared up to this point that this may be their opportunity.

Praying Together.

As stated last week, the effectiveness of this group and the quality of relationship will be enhanced by a commitment to pray for each other by name each day. If you have pictures of each other, as requested last week, put these pictures face down on a table and let each person select a picture. This person will be the focus of special prayer for the week. Bring the photos back next week, shuffle them and draw again. Continue this throughout your pilgrimage together. Looking at a person's picture as you pray for that person will add meaning. Having the picture will also remind you that you are to give special prayer attention to this person during the week.

1. Praying corporately each week is a special ministry. Take some time now for a period of verbal prayer, allowing each person to mention any special needs he or she wishes to share with the entire group.

A good pattern is to ask for a period of prayer after each need is mentioned. There may be silent prayer by the entire group, or someone may offer a brief two-or-three-sentence verbal prayer.

2. Close your time by praying together the great prayer of the church, "Our Father." As you pray this prayer, remember that you are linking yourselves with all Christians of all time in universal intercession.

Words of Encouragement

As you begin this third week of your journey, here are some thoughts to keep in mind.

Discipline is an important dimension of life. Discipline is not slavish rigidity but an ordering of life that enables you to control your circumstances rather than being controlled by them. For most people, a designated time of prayer is essential for building a life of prayer.

If you have not yet established a regular time to use this workbook and as your prayer time, try to find the right time for you this week. Experiment: in the morning, after work, during the lunch hour, before retiring. Find time that seems best for you.

If you discover that you can't cover all the workbook material and exercises given for a day, don't berate yourself. Get what you can out of what you do. There is no point in rushing over three or four steps or principles if you cannot think deeply. Consider them seriously one by one, and move only as far as you can.

Intellectual assent to a great principle or possibility is important, but it does us little good until we act upon it—until we say yes in our minds, and live it out in relationships.

Don't hesitate to make decisions and resolves, but don't condemn yourself if you fail. God is patient and wants us to be patient with ourselves.

An Affirming Presence

Day One: *Death for Deadness*

Last week we focused on Paul's concept of death and resurrection as the image of the Christian life—dying and rising *in Christ*. Paul provides a profound expression of this in his letter to the Romans. "You are not in the flesh, you are in the Spirit, if in fact the Spirit of God dwells in you. Any one who does not have the Spirit of Christ does not belong to him. But if Christ is in you, although your bodies are dead because of sin, your spirits are alive because of righteousness" (Rom. 8:9–11, RSV).

This passage is a kind of summing up of Paul's sharing about his own personal struggle, which is also universal—the struggle with our sinful nature. How intimately we identify with his expression: "I do not do the good I want, but the evil I do not want is what I do" (Rom. 7:19, RSV).

Apart from physical death, there are two kinds of death for Paul.

One was inevitable; Paul might even say involuntary. We are dead in sin; this is the plight of all. Dominated by sin, our life is a living death. Then comes a choice to die. We choose to die to sin, to "the elemental spirits of the universe" (Col. 2:20), and so our "life is hid with Christ in God" (Col. 3:3). This choosing to die is a negative movement; we voluntarily die to our "old" nature, to the flesh which for Paul means not our body, but a domain of power in which unredeemed human nature is in control. That is only a part of the matter. We *come alive* to God in Jesus Christ. We share the resurrection of our Lord.

As we grow in being alive in Christ, every part of our life is

63

connected with Christ. We live *in* Christ (Col. 2:6), and *with* Christ (Col. 2:13). We are instructed by Christ; his word dwells in us (Col. 3:16). Our relationship with Christ shapes our relationship with others. Christ within us forms the atmosphere in which we live. To the degree of our yieldedness to the indwelling Christ we manifest his presence in the world. (*AC,* pp. 49–50).

That brings us back almost to where we began. On Day Three of Week One, you were asked to memorize this statement of truth: The presence of God in Jesus Christ is to be experienced not only on occasion, but the indwelling Christ is to become the shaping power of our lives. *Our opportunity is to choose death over deadness.* That is, we voluntarily choose to die with Christ to a domain of power in which our unredeemed nature is in control and to live *in* Christ and *with* Christ, so that he becomes the shaping power of our lives.

Reflecting and Recording

From this point on in our workbook journey, we will be concentrating on the shaping power of the indwelling Christ, hopefully opening and yielding ourselves to this extravagant possibility. Ponder for a few minutes some different expressions of this option that is ours.

Abide in me, and I in you. As the branch cannot bear fruit by itself, unless it abides in the vine, neither can you, unless you abide in me.
—John 15:4, RSV

Oh, my dear children, I feel the pangs of childbirth all over again till Christ be formed within you.
—Galatians 4:19, PHILLIPS

I have been crucified with Christ; it is no longer I who live, but Christ who lives in me; and the life I now live in the flesh I live by faith in the Son of God, who loved me and gave himself for me.
—Galatians 2:20, RSV

. . . until we all attain to the unity of the faith and of the knowledge of the Son of God, to mature manhood, to the measure of the stature of the fulness of Christ.
—Ephesians 4:13, RSV

Him we proclaim, warning every man and teaching every man in all wisdom, that we may present every man mature in Christ.
—Colossians 1:28, RSV

. . . and to know [the love of God], though it is beyond knowledge. So may you attain to fullness of being, the fullness of God himself.

—Ephesians 3:19, NEB

Now write a prayer expressing your desire and commitment to be formed in Christ, shaped by him to be all that God wants you to be—God's "fullness of being" for you. Make this a time of reflection on where you are now and where you would like to be in your spiritual life, a time to examine your willingness to change, how free you are to risk, to yield yourself to the shaping power of the indwelling Christ. Writing your prayer will help you in your reflection and will assist you in finding clarity and being specific.

During the Day

Select your favorite from verses above that give expression to the possibility of your being shaped by Christ, memorize that verse, and call it to mind throughout the day as a reminder of the prayer you have just written and prayed.

Day Two: *A Personal Confession*

The focus of this week is the indwelling Christ as an *affirming presence*. A desperate need!

In my pastoral experience, I don't believe I have discovered a more common malady crippling people and stifling their growth in Christ than varying expressions of *worthlessness*. We will talk more in the days ahead about how this expresses itself. But today I want to witness to the tenacious hold these feelings, or a mind-set of worthlessness, can have on us by a personal confession.

In my book, *Dancing at My Funeral,* I plotted my early spiritual journey which centered in large part on this struggle for self-worth, a battle against self-pity and self-deprecation.

Coming from a poverty-bound situation in rural Mississippi, I was economically, educationally, and socially deprived. The passion of my life was to overcome the limitations of that deprivation. I became a driven person, an almost hopeless workaholic, a tough taskmaster of myself—wanting to perform, to achieve, to gain status. I drove myself mercilessly to prove myself worthy to be accepted by God and by others. Along the way, I did learn a very hard lesson—that to love and accept on the basis of worthiness is not worthy of being called love and acceptance. Love cannot be dependent upon worthiness. To accept another on the basis of performance is a superficial sham.

I thought I had won the battle, and to a marked degree I had, but about five years ago, it ravaged my spirit again in a rather subtle but telling way.

Douglas Steere, the great Quaker scholar and champion of the inner life who has written so helpfully on prayer and spirituality, came to The Upper Room for one of our monthly conferences. He and I spent a marvelous afternoon together. To be in the presence of this spiritual giant was a challenging, freeing, illuminating experience. For three consecutive years Dr. Steere had invited me to share in The Ecumenical Institute of Spirituality. This is a small group of twenty-five people—many of them the stature of Dr. Steere—who gather once a year for three days to hear prepared papers, to dialogue on chosen themes, and to share their spiritual pilgrimages with each other.

Every year I had refused the invitation, telling myself I was too busy, that other engagements were more important, even making commitments for the time of the meeting of the institute in order to have a clear excuse. When Dr. Steere pressed the invitation again, the Spirit confronted me with the truth about myself. I did not feel adequate or worthy to be in that distinguished company; and my neurotic need to be completely adequate, to be secure, to be accepted was the reason I had turned down the invitation. Well, bless Dr. Steere! He ministered to me. He helped me see that I was reacting to that opportunity and challenge not out of the self that was seeking to grow, not out of the self that was yielding itself to the shaping power of the indwelling Christ, but that I was slinking back into that shriveled person of self-pity and self-depreciation, hiding in my feelings of inadequacy and unworthiness.

I sought to deal with those feelings decisively again by allowing the indwelling Christ to affirm me and give me the power to overcome those feelings of inadequacy, insecurity, and unworthiness. I've been a part of The Ecumenical Institute of Spirituality now for seven years, and our annual meeting is one of the richest experiences of my life.

I still wrestle with the problem. Now and then it comes to the fore and plays havoc with my sense of well-being and wholeness. I deal with it by claiming the affirming presence of Christ.

Reflecting and Recording

One of the most affirming words of Jesus came when he was teaching about the meaning of discipleship. He put *fear* in this perspective:

> Do not fear those who kill the body but cannot kill the soul; rather fear him who can destroy both soul and body in hell. Are not two sparrows sold for a penny? And not one of them will fall to the ground without your Father's will. But even the hairs of your head are all numbered. Fear not, therefore; you are of more value than many sparrows.
> —Matthew 10:28–31, RSV

Does that cause your soul to stand on tiptoe? "The hairs of your head are numbered." No sparrow falls without the Father noting it. "You are of more value than many sparrows."

Think of this affirmation of Jesus against the backdrop of my personal confession. What prevents us from claiming the affirming presence of Christ? How do we lose sight of who we are as God's own children, known personally by God?" Where are you in the struggle against feelings of worthlessness? Stay with those questions for a while, and claim to whatever degree you can what it means that with God "even the hairs of your head are all numbered."

✳ ✳ ✳

During the Day

In your encounters with others today, be attentive to the dynamics of relationships. Be sensitive to feelings of worthlessness on your part or on the part of those with whom you are sharing. Try to move the dynamic of relationship to mutual acceptance.

On page 173, you will find a tent-card cutout with this affirmation: To love and accept on the basis of worthiness is not worthy of being called love and acceptance. Cut out, fold on marked line, set on your desk or table as a reminder of the unconditional love we are to give and receive.

Day Three: *A Spiritual Disease*

I said yesterday that in my pastoral experience I have not discovered a more common malady crippling people and stifling their growth in Christ than varying expressions of worthlessness. Today, let's name it for what it is—a spiritual disease:

- a disease that works on our minds, distorting our vision of reality.
- a disease that attacks our spirits, sapping our spiritual energy.
- a disease that engages our emotions, poisoning our feelings.
- a disease that always makes us neurotic because it fills us with fear and anxiety.
- a disease which can make us psychotic because, if allowed to run its course, feelings of worthlessness turn into suspicion and hatred of others.

There are degrees of disease-seriousness, which we identify by various names: lack of self-worth, self-pity, low self-esteem, self-depreciation, little or no self-affirmation. Self-hatred is the extreme expression. Many people who commit suicide have become the victims of this disease. Most of us, when we are honest, recognize its crippling power in our lives and many confess it as a ravaging debilitation.

The problem expresses itself in a variety of ways: through lack of confidence, through fear and anxiety about performance. We never feel we measure up.

It is easier, perhaps, to identify it and talk about it in others than in ourselves. People do a marvelous job, and we commend them. Rather than accepting commendation, they begin to point out the imperfections and failures in their performance. Because they don't believe in themselves, they can't believe that we believe in them. Because they can't affirm themselves, they have difficulty accepting our affirmation.

Self-pity and self-depreciation are also expressed as jealousy and envy. We harbor thoughts and feelings that others are more blessed than we. We see only the surface of other's lives, and we become resentful and keep asking, "Why couldn't I have been so lucky?"

It grows in us because we focus on the chasm between our *ideal* and our *real* self, the vast distance between who and what we would like to be and who and what we know we are. We know with Paul that the good we would do we do not; and the evil we would not, that we do. Therefore we continue in despair: "Wretched man that I am!" (Rom. 7:24, RSV). For some of us, it comes as a kind of midlife crisis, an oppression of spirit because we have not realized our dreams, and we are overcome with the morbid thought that we never will.

Enough description and diagnosis—what about a prescription, an answer?

Self-affirmation comes when we accept the fact that God knows us thoroughly and yet loves us completely. This is a part of the shaping power of the indwelling Christ. He is an affirming presence, reminding us that God knows us thoroughly, and yet loves us completely. Remember Jesus' word:

> Therefore I tell you, do not be anxious about your life, what you shall eat or what you shall drink, nor about your body, what you shall put on. Is not life more than food, and the body more than clothing? Look at the birds of the air: they neither sow nor reap nor gather into barns, and yet your heavenly Father feeds them. Are you not of more value than they?
> —Matthew 6: 25–26, RSV

Reflecting and Recording

Yesterday in the reflecting and recording period you were asked to begin thinking about where you are in your struggle against feelings of worthlessness. What prevents us from claiming the affirming presence of Christ? When the witness of scripture is that God knows and loves us, why do we continue to be made powerless by self-pity? Write here your ''confession'' of struggle with feelings of worthlessness.

During the Day

Continue your attentiveness to the dynamics of relationship in your encounters. Did you work on it yesterday? Were there specific instances where feelings of worthlessness were present? Be observant today and try to move the dynamic of relationship to mutual acceptance.

Day Four: *Spirit and Flesh*

There is therefore now no condemnation for those who are in Christ Jesus. For the law of the Spirit of life in Christ Jesus has set me free from the law of sin and death. For God has done what the law, weakened by the flesh, could not do: sending his own Son in the likeness of sinful flesh and for sin, he condemned sin in the flesh, in order that the just requirement of the law might be fulfilled in us, who walk not according to the flesh but according to the Spirit. For those who live according to the flesh set their minds on the things of the flesh, but those who live according to the Spirit set their minds on the things of the Spirit. To set the mind on the flesh is death, but to set the mind on the Spirit is life and peace. For the mind that is set on the flesh is hostile to God; it does not submit to God's law, indeed it cannot; and those who are in the flesh cannot please God.

But you are not in the flesh, you are in the Spirit, if in fact the Spirit of God dwells in you. Any one who does not have the Spirit of Christ does not belong to him. But if Christ is in you, although your bodies are dead because of sin, your spirits are alive because of righteousness. If the Spirit of him who raised Jesus from the dead dwells in you, he who raised Christ Jesus from the dead will give life to your mortal bodies also through his Spirit which dwells in you.

—Romans 8:1–11, RSV

Life is often seen as a struggle between spirit and flesh. There has been a great deal of confusion and misunderstanding, often leading to a condemnation of our bodies. This has led to body-denying, world-denying spiritualities. These spiritualities equate body and flesh and thus the primary "spiritual" disciplines are focused on bringing the "body" under subjection. This view of spirituality is limited, at best, and perverted at its worst.

Paul is the New Testament writer around whom this confusion and misunderstanding swirl because he talked so much about spirit and flesh. We can't deal extensively with this theme or give a full exposition of Paul's biblical teaching here. However, it is helpful to clarify one point about Paul's teaching in the context of this focus on the indwelling Christ as an affirming presence.

At the heart of Paul's witness was his passionate belief that we are called into being by God at creation, and we are called into *new being* by God at redemption through Jesus Christ. Our redemption, our new-being status, is not a static state but a pilgrimage, a path opened to us by Jesus, "the pioneer and perfecter of our faith" (Heb. 12:2, RSV).

"The life I now live in the flesh" (Gal. 2:20) is Paul's reference to his whole self. Setting flesh against spirit is a distortion of Paul's teaching. Also, to equate Paul's use of the word *flesh* with the substance of the body as we see it is a mistake. (He used two different words: *sarx* meaning flesh, and *sōma* meaning body.)

For Paul, as Spirit (spelled with a capital S) is a domain of power, so is flesh a domain of power, a sphere of influence in which one lives.

For Paul, to live "in the flesh" was to live as a member of human society in a physical body.

Now comes the important issue.

It is important to see clearly that Paul did not equate flesh and sin. The only passage in which it might appear that he did is in Romans 8:3 where the incarnation is seen as "God . . . sending his own Son in the likeness of sinful flesh . . ." and "condemned sin in the flesh." "Sinful flesh" appears to characterize flesh itself as sinful while "condemned sin in the flesh" distinguishes flesh from sin. The latter is true to Paul's understanding. Sin is linked closely to flesh because flesh is the domain of power where sin operates. Sin, not flesh, is condemned. God came in Christ to enter the domain of power, the flesh, in order that sin might be conquered once and for all. Our predicament is not that we are *in the flesh,* but that we are in sin, that is, living according to, setting our minds on flesh rather than the spirit, as a domain of power.

With this understanding, Paul's affirmation makes sense and is the call for us: "The life I now live in the flesh I live by faith in the Son of God, who loved me and gave Himself for me."

We are *In the flesh* and will be until we die. To be in the flesh is not to be in sin, but to live "according to the flesh" is to be in sin. Spirit is the power-sphere of the new age. Living "by faith in the Son of God" is to live in Spirit, not to have the norms and values of our life shaped by the frail, vulnerable transient nature of flesh, but to be in a new realm, the Kingdom of Spirit, where power is ours from the indwelling Christ, and hope is ours because of his resurrection (Dunnam, *The Communicator's Commentary,* pp. 51–52).

Reality for Christians includes a realm of Spirit that is as real as the realm of flesh (material). A person is a being consisting of physical, mental, emotional and spiritual aspects. As human beings, we are, therefore, body, mind, heart (the seat of our emotion), and soul. Our wholeness depends on the growth and development of all these aspects. Health or "dis-ease" in one aspect of our being may affect the health of any other part or of the whole.

Later on, we will focus in a special way on keeping the conversion process alive. What we need to nail down in our thinking now is that Christ is not at war with us as persons. Who we are, including our bodies, our drives and instincts and passions, is not to be negated or despised, but affirmed.

Reflecting and Recording

Remembering that flesh and Spirit are both domains of power, look at your life during the past months. Focus especially on decisions you wrestled with, relationships in which you had to invest a good bit of time and energy. Can you identify any struggles between flesh and ''Spirit''? Describe at least two of those here.

During the Day

Be conscious of the possibility of flesh vying with Spirit for control in your life today. Try to see that everything your *body,* your total physical being, wants to do is not the flesh at work.

Day Five: *You Are of More Value than Sparrows*

Yesterday I asked you to be conscious of flesh vying with Spirit for control in your life. Were you able to distinguish between flesh as a domain of power and your *body,* your total physical being?

✳   ✳   ✳

The indwelling Christ does not condemn our physical being. Our drives and passions are sometimes referred to as *carnal* and are condemned by some religious teaching. It is as though our *human nature* is evil. Not so. Christ was not at war with human nature. In our commitment to ''grow up in Christ'' we must always remember that there is a difference between discipline and denial. We don't deny our human self. (In fact, there is no other self than a human one.) We don't deny or suppress or seek to destroy our drives and passions. We discipline them to serve our goal of being *in Christ*. We recognize the need for our drives and passions to be redeemed by the indwelling Christ.

We will come back to this in Week 6. For now it is to be noted because who we are, our total life, body, mind, heart and soul is affirmed by Christ. Once again, pay attention to Jesus' words—this time recorded in the Gospel of Luke:

> I tell you, my friends, do not fear those who kill the body, and after that have no more that they can do. But I will warn you whom to fear: fear him who, after he has killed, has power to cast into hell; yes, I tell you, fear him! Are not five sparrows sold for two pennies? And not one of them is forgotten before God. Why, even the hairs of your head are all numbered. Fear not; you are of more value than many sparrows.
>
> —Luke 12:4–7, RSV

There is a story about Oliver Wendell Holmes going out for a walk one day near his summer home. A little girl joined him for a time. When she said she had to go home, her distinguished companion said, ''When you mother asks you where you have been, tell her you've been walking with Oliver Wendell Holmes.''

Without hesitation, the little girl replied, ''And when your folks ask you where you have been, tell them you were walking with Mary Susanna Brown.''

It was a spontaneous response flowing out of a healthy sense of confidence and esteem. I wish it were *natural*. It isn't. Unfortunately, most persons feel worthless rather than valuable.

The indwelling Christ affirms our being, builds in us a healthy sense of importance. Not the arrogant self-importance that seeks to lord it over others and allows us to think more highly of ourselves than we ought to think, but the knowledge of who we are: God's children, loved by God, valued—the hairs on our heads numbered.

Reflecting and Recording

Locate in your memory an experience with another person or persons in which you felt intimidated, embarrassed, put down, impotent, out of control. Make enough notes here about that experience to get it clearly in mind.

Focus on yourself in that experience. Why were you intimidated? What made you feel put down or out of control? Were you embarrassed because you did not have strength to act or the courage to respond? *What role did your own feelings of self-worth, or the lack of it,* play in the situation? Think about that for a moment.

❋   ❋   ❋

Suppose you could have responded as Mary Susanna Brown did to Oliver Wendell Holmes: would there have been a difference?

❋   ❋   ❋

During the Day

In all your relationships today, remember Mary Susanna Brown, and Jesus' words: "Why, even the hairs of your head are all numbered. Fear not; you are of more value than many sparrows" (Luke 12:7, RSV).

Day Six: *Experiencing Being Valuable*

Emmaus is a movement started by The Upper Room based on the Cursillo of the Roman Catholic Church. At the heart of it is a seventy-two-hour experience of persons living together in community, hearing numerous talks all centered on the grace of God, seeking to appropriate the meaning of that core message of Christianity by dialoguing in small table groups, praying and worshiping together, celebrating Holy Communion, and spending time in silence reflecting on the meaning of God's grace in our personal lives. This seventy-two-hour "Walk to Emmaus" closes with the participants having the opportunity to share what they have personally experienced during the seventy-two hours and how they intend to incorporate their experience into the whole of their lives.

The most common experience shared by participants in this "Walk to Emmaus" is that of becoming overwhlemingly aware of God's love and acceptance.

Psychologists and psychiatrists tell us that being valuable is absolutely essential to mental health, and we feel valuable only with a healthy self-image. A healthy self-image is gained in childhood, primarily as a direct result of parental love. If not acquired in childhood, it comes slowly, painfully, and often by dramatic intervention of love or conversion in adult life.

I've seen this intervention of love leading to conversion and a restoration of a healthy self-image over and over in Emmaus.

I was moved to tears of sadness and joy recently as a young woman, six months pregnant with her second child, through stifled sobs shared her experience. She had come to Emmaus an emotional wreck. Had I not known some of her same feelings, and had I not spent countless hours counseling with people in the same ravaging destructive dilemma, I would have found it extremely difficult to believe her confession. She was a beautiful person, alive in personality, attractive in every way, having all those things the world counts important going for her. Yet she said something like this: "I have felt ugly inside, unworthy, undeserving of the love of my husband and my little boy. I've had horrible thoughts about how I'm going to love this little one soon to be born because I feel so unlovable and incapable of love myself."

She smiled broadly through her tears, her face was radiant and her eyes danced with joy as she said that during the weekend she had, for the first time in her life, accepted the fact that God loved her unconditionally—that the presence of Christ in the community had become real in her own life, affirming her, and she could go home to accept the love of her husband and son, and wait with joyous anticipation the birth of her new child, knowing that she would be worthy of that child's love, and could love the child without reservation (*AC,* p. 60).

Consider the incredible love that the Father has shown us in allowing us
to be called "children of God"—and that is not just what we are called,
but what we *are*. This explains why the world will no more recognize us
than it recognizes Christ.

Here and now, my dear friends, we *are* God's children. We don't
know what we shall become in the future. We only know that, when he
appears we shall be like him, for we shall see him as he really is!

Everyone who has at heart a hope like that keeps himself pure, as Christ
is pure.

—1 John 3:1–3, PHILIPPS

The witness of scripture is that God wants all of us to experience
God's love. That's what the young woman experienced at Emmaus,
and it was a *conversion*.

Reflecting and Recording

Name two or three persons with whom you share who are suffering
from low self-esteem, not feeling valuable. Put their names on the
lines:

_____

_____

_____

_____

Look at each of these. Do you know them well enough to know why
they do not feel valuable? Make some notes beside each name. Are
there people who express love to them? Are they a part of a Christian
community where love and acceptance prevail? Do you know anything about their childhood? What can you do to demonstrate God's
love to them? Write your response beside each name.

✳   ✳   ✳

During the Day

Act today to demonstrate God's love through you to the persons you listed.

Day Seven: *God Knows Us Thoroughly and Loves Us Thoroughly*

The love and acceptance of God is kept alive in our lives by the indwelling Christ. Paul wrote the new Christians in Colossae, "Just as you received Christ, so go on living in him—in simple faith. Grow out of him as a plant grows out of the soil it is planted in, becoming more and more sure of the faith as you were taught it, and your lives will overflow with joy and thankfulness" (Col. 2:6–7, PHILLIPS).

Our unfortunate situation is that to experience the love and acceptance of God on occasion is not enough. What is the key then? *Self-affirmation comes when we accept the fact that God knows us thoroughly and loves us thoroughly. Knowing that we are pardoned, accepted, and affirmed by God is the dynamic that makes possible our acceptance of ourselves.*

M. Scott Peck, the popular psychiatrist who wrote *The Road Less Traveled* and *People of the Lie,* connects a good self-image and self-discipline. In fact, he contends that the feeling of being valuable is the cornerstone of self-discipline. When we consider ourselves valuable we will take care of ourselves in all the ways necessary. "Self-discipline is self-caring."

We apply this to our understanding of the discipline of spiritual formation: "receiving through faith and appropriating through commitment, discipline, and action, the living Christ into our own life to the end that our life will conform to, and manifest the reality of Christ's presence in the world."

This is that to which Paul was calling us: "Just as you received Christ, so go on living in him."

Our Christian faith journey begins with our acceptance of the incredible fact of our unconditional acceptance by God. Nothing we can do can earn or prove our worth. Our value in God's sight has been affirmed once and for all by the gift of Jesus Christ in death on our behalf. We continue on our Christian journey, as forgiven and affirmed people, as we allow our lives to be shaped by the indwelling Christ who keeps affirming us in our worth and impelling us to "fullness of being, the fullness of God himself" (*AC*, p. 61).

Reflecting and Recording

Yesterday, you were asked to name persons who are suffering from low self-esteem, not feeling valuable. Think about your own self. Sometimes looking at others helps us see ourselves. Ask yourself: Do I feel valuable? Have I accepted the fact that God knows me thoroughly and loves me thoroughly? Am I allowing the fact that someone doesn't love and accept me to block my acceptance of God's love?

Spend a few minutes looking at your own life, then write a word of response to God's love.

How does what you have experienced and written fit into the statement that self-affirmation comes when we accept the fact that God knows us thoroughly and loves us thoroughly?

✳ ✳ ✳

During the Day

Don't forget if you are a part of a group that your group meeting is tonight.

Continue your action to demonstrate God's love through you to those persons you listed yesterday.

Be sensitive to whether other people's failure to affirm you causes you to question your self-worth and God's love.

Group Meeting for Week Three

Note: The leader for this week should bring a chalkboard or newsprint to the group meeting. See suggestion six of direction for group sharing below.

Introduction

Two essential ingredients of a Christian fellowship are *feedback* and *follow-up*. Feedback is necessary to keep the group dynamic working positively for all participants. Follow-up is essential to express Christian concern and ministry.

The leader is primarily responsible for feedback in the group. All persons should be encouraged to share their feelings about how the group is functioning. Listening is crucial. To listen to another, as much as any other action, is a means of affirming that person. When we listen to another, we are saying, "You are important; I value you." It is also crucial to check out meaning in order that those who are sharing this pilgrimage may know that we really hear. We often mis-hear. "Are you saying———?" is a good check question. It takes only a couple of persons in a group, who listen and give feedback in this fashion, to set the mood for the group.

Follow-up is the function of everyone. If we listen to what others are saying, we will discover needs and concerns beneath the surface, situations that deserve special prayer and attention. Make notes of these as the group shares. Follow up during the week with a telephone call, a written note of caring and encouragement, a visit. What distinguishes a Christian fellowship is *caring in action*. "My, how those Christians love one another!"

So follow up each week with others in the group.

Sharing Together

By this time, a significant amount of "knowing" exists in the group. Persons are feeling safe in the group, perhaps more willing to share. Still, there is no place for pressure. The leader, however, should be especially sensitive to those slow to share. Seek gently to coax them out. Every person is a gift to the group. The gift is fully revealed by sharing.

1. Begin your meeting with a time of prayer. Ask two or three persons to share the prayers they wrote on Day One of this week. It will be helpful if the leader asks some persons ahead of time to do this.

2. On Day Two of this week, I shared my confession of struggle with the matter of self-esteem. Invite persons in the group to share their struggles. Take as much time as necessary for all to share, each person taking as much as three minutes if needed.

3. Take five to ten minutes to discuss the statement: "Self-affirmation comes when we accept the fact that God knows us thoroughly and loves us thoroughly." Focus on what prevents us from believing and claiming this.

4. Invite two or three persons to share their struggles between *flesh* and *Spirit* as considered on Day Four. After the sharing of experiences, ask the group to talk about this whole idea of *realms of power* which vie for our allegiance. Is this a new idea? Is it clear? What are big questions unanswered in the text or in your mind?

5. On Day Five I told the story of Oliver Wendell Holmes and Mary Susanna Brown. Ask two or three persons to describe some Mary Susanna Browns they know. What characterizes their lives? What is the source of their self-confidence? In your discussion, try to connect the sharing about these persons with the experiences of intimidation, being put down, embarrassed, or feeling out of control that persons were asked to record in their reflection period on Day Five.

6. Ask everyone to turn to p. 77 of their workbook where they listed names of persons suffering from low self-esteem. Looking at the data there and using the chalkboard or newsprint the leader brought, make a list of that which causes people to feel worthless. Concentrate on causes.

✳ ✳ ✳

Now let the group talk about what can be done for persons to enable them to overcome feelings of low self-esteem and rejection. List these here and on the newsprint or chalkboard.

Ask each person now to look at this list in light of the persons they named on Day Six. Is there something from this list you might practice in relation to the persons to whom you want to demonstrate God's love? Make some notes here.

Praying Together

1. The leader should take up the polaroid pictures of the group, shuffle them, and let each person draw a new one.

2. Invite each member of the group to spend two minutes in quiet prayer for the person whose picture he or she had drawn, focusing on what the person has shared in this meeting.

3. Close the time with sentence prayers, praying specifically about the needs shared by persons when they talked about their struggle with the matter of self-esteem and/or the battle between flesh and Spirit.

Week Four

A Forgiving and Healing Presence

Day One: *A Picture of the Father*

[Jesus] said, "There was a man who had two sons; and the younger of them said to his father, 'Father, give me the share of property that falls to me.' And he divided his living between them. Not many days later, the younger son gathered all he had and took his journey into a far country, and there he squandered his property in loose living. And when he had spent everything, a great famine arose in that country, and he began to be in want. So he went and joined himself to one of the citizens of that country, who sent him into his fields to feed swine. And he would gladly have fed on the pods that the swine ate; and no one gave him anything. But when he came to himself he said, 'How many of my father's hired servants have bread enough and to spare, but I perish here with hunger! I will arise and go to my father, and I will say to him, "Father, I have sinned against heaven and before you; I am no longer worthy to be called your son; treat me as one of your hired servants."' And he arose and came to his father. But while he was yet at a distance, his father saw him and had compassion, and ran and embraced him and kissed him. And the son said to him, 'Father, I have sinned against heaven and before you; I am no longer worthy to be called your son.' But the father said to his servants, 'Bring quickly the best robe, and put it on him; and put a ring on his hand, and shoes on his feet; and bring the fatted calf and kill it, and let us eat and make merry; for this is my son who was dead, and is alive again; he was lost, and is found.' And they began to make merry.

—Luke 15:11–24, RSV

There are many lessons here—enough to occupy Bible students in every generation, enough to demand hours of reflection at any serious time of consideration.

85

But what is the primary lesson? Boil it down, refine it to its most precious essence, and I believe the central truth of the parable is this: *When the prodigal son returned home, his father received him as though he had never been away.*

That's grace! Though Jesus teaches us a lot in the parable, he gives us a picture of God. There is no mistaking the point: God's grace is a forgiving grace.

In *Take Effective Control of Your Life,* psychiatrist William Glasser says that the power of pictures in our minds is a total power. We all have in our minds hundreds and even thousands of pictures that will satisfy our needs. We must have at least one picture for every need.

Jesus must have known the power pictures have in our lives. So he gave us the picture of God as the loving father who receives his wayward son home as though he had never been away—embraces the son in forgiveness, places the family ring on his finger, gives him the signs of love and hospitality—a clean robe and sandals—and celebrates with a party.

Reflecting and Recording

What is the dominant picture of God you have in your mind? Spend a few minutes thinking about your image of God.

❋   ❋   ❋

When the prodigal son returned home his father received him as though he had never been away. Can you locate any experience in your life when some other person responded to you in that fashion? Describe your experience here. Write enough to get in touch with and relive your experience.

❋   ❋   ❋

Have you ever experienced God in that way? Write a brief description of that experience.

During the Day

In your activity and relationships today, try to think about how pictures in your mind are determining your action and response.

In my introduction to the last week's group sharing session, I talked about the importance of *follow-up*. You were asked to make notes of persons and situations that deserve special attention and prayer, and to make telephone calls, write notes of care and encouragement, or visit persons. Begin today to act on the notes you made—and *follow-up* this week with members of your group. You be Christ's affirming presence needed by someone.

Day Two: *A Picture of Jesus*

William Glasser, the best-selling author-psychiatrist, to whom we referred yesterday, says that the power of the pictures in our heads is total.

In our relentless efforts to satisfy them, we may go so far as to choose behaviors that endanger our lives. For centuries parents have become distraught when a teen-age daughter chooses to stop eating and begins to starve to death. It is still called by its ancient Latin label, anorexia nervosa—loss of appetite for no known physical reason. Some understanding of this crazy choice not to eat can be gleaned through the concept of the picture albums in our heads. A researcher who did an ingenious experiment with anorexics showed them pictures depicting their heads superimposed on a series of bodies ranging from what most of us would call ''normal'' all the way to skeletal. Then he asked the young women, ''Which of the bodies do you like seeing your head attached to?'' To the researcher's surprise, they said none of them—all were too fat. What they were saying was that they wanted to be thinner than whatever they saw in the mirror. To achieve this irrational degree of thinness, they had no choice but to starve themselves, and they did'' (Glasser, p. 23).

If Glasser is right, and I believe he is, how essential it is that we make vivid in our minds the picture of the forgiving Christ. Remember that part of our definition of spiritual formation? ''Cultivating awareness of . . . the indwelling Christ.''

Here is an action picture from scripture:

Early next morning, [Jesus] returned to the Temple and the entire crowd came to him. So he sat down and began to teach them. But the scribes and Pharisees brought in to him a woman who had been caught in adultery. They made her stand in front, and then said to him, ''Now, Master, this woman has been caught in adultery, in the very act. According to the Law, Moses commanded us to stone such women to death. Now, what do you say about her?''

They said this to test him, so that they might have some good grounds for an accusation. But Jesus stooped down and began to write with his finger in the dust on the ground. But as they persisted in their questioning, he straightened himself up and said to them, ''Let the one among you who has never sinned throw the first stone at her.'' Then he stooped down again and continued writing with his finger on the ground. And when they heard what he said, they were convicted by their own consciences and went out, one by one, beginning with the eldest until they had all gone.

Jesus was left alone, with the woman still standing where they had put her. So he stood up and said to her, ''Where are they all—did no one condemn you?''

And she said, ''No one, sir.''

''Neither do I condemn you,'' said Jesus to her. ''Go home and do not sin again.''

—John 8:1–11, PHILLIPS

I sat for two hours recently with one of my dearest friends. She and her husband were members of the congregation I organized my first year out of seminary. Our relationship has been a lively one through these twenty-plus years. My wife and I always felt theirs was a model marriage. Love abounded. Within the family the expression of affection was spontaneous and free. They had three boys, again models of happiness, growth, and togetherness.

I had not seen my friend for a year. I knew from our correspondence that a recent family event was devastating. One of her sons was going through his second divorce, and he was less than thirty years old. Another son had divorced five years previously. My friend—I think illegitimately but nevertheless genuinely—is overwhelmed with guilt. Her big question, What did we do or fail to do in relation to our boys? Three divorces in a family is a pretty heavy load.

I tried to convince her of the power of Christ to lift that burden of guilt. Even if she did have some responsibility in the matter, God forgives. *The indwelling Christ is a forgiving presence,* making us aware of a double need in our lives—the need to be forgiven, and the need to forgive others. As a living presence in our lives, Christ continues the ministry he not only preached but practiced during his earthly life (*AC*, p. 65).

Reflecting and Recording

Examine your conscience now. It is so essential that you take enough time and probe deeply enough to identify the actual situation. Do you feel guilt? Is there an uneasiness in you because something is wrong in your relationship with a loved one or friend? Are you spiritually "dis-eased" because you are guilty for unconfessed, unforgiven sins because you have not deliberately sought and received Christ's forgiveness?

Make notes in response to these questions. Be as honest and specific as you can. Name events, persons, experiences, and situations. There is additional space on the next page.

Now ask yourself this question. Since Jesus treated the adulteress with such respect and forgiving love, why can't I trust him to treat me in the same fashion?

❋   ❋   ❋

What is preventing me from receiving that forgiveness?

❋   ❋   ❋

During the Day

Remember our primary thesis in the first two weeks of this study—that Christ dwells in our hearts through faith, that the meaning of the Christian life is to live *in Christ*. The presence of God in Christ is to be experienced not only on occasion, but the indwelling Christ is to become the shaping power of our lives.

Today, take the picture of Christ forgiving the woman taken in adultery as your picture of the indwelling Christ, a forgiving presence for you, but also a reminder of your need to forgive others.

Day Three: *Good News, Bad News, Good News*

"Therefore, if any one is in Christ, he is a new creation; the old has passed away, behold, the new has come" (2 Cor. 5:17, RSV).

Spend a minute or two reflecting on the radical claim Paul is making here.

❋   ❋   ❋

The gospel of Jesus Christ involves good news, bad news, good news. That we are created in the image of God is the first *good news*. At creation, Adam and Eve were in fellowship with God, without shame, or guilt, or fear. *Original righteousness* we sometimes call it.

The *bad news* is that we lost that God-created image. Adam and Eve sinned. They disobeyed God, chose their own way rather than listening to and obeying God. Since then we humans have had a propensity to evil; we call it *original sin*. Sin cannot bear the light of God, so, like Adam and Eve, we continue to hide.

In the Old Testament, God provided a temporary covering for sin. This was a covenant God made with Israel. The covenant was renewed each year as the high priest went into the holy of holies to make the sacrifice of blood on the mercy seat which covered the ark of the covenant. God then initiated a new covenant—*the second good news*. "God so loved the world that he gave his only you son" (John 3:16, RSV). This was a new covenant of grace, not a temporary covering (*propitiation*) for sin but a permanent solution, to root our (*expiate*) sins. Thus Paul could say: "Therefore, if any one is in Christ, he is a new creation; the old has passed away, behold, the new has come" (2 Cor. 5:17 RSV).

Good news, bad news, good news. All three of these aspects of the gospel are essential. Robert Tuttle, Jr. has said it well:

> Some omit the first good news. Their gospel is simply bad news/good news. Salvation, however, is far more than the forgiveness of sins; it is restoring us to our original righteousness—"without holiness no one will see the Lord." Others omit the bad news. Their gospel is simply good news/good news. They refuse to believe that our sin is serious enough to warrant separation from God or man. Still others omit both the bad news and the second good news. In this instance good news without bad news is no news. They believe that there is no need for reconciliation since God is "all loving" and would not allow our sins to cause separation in the first place (Tuttle, p. 29).

I interject this brief theological statement here to underscore the connection between forgiveness and restoration, or healing. To be alive in Christ is to be whole as the persons God intended us to be.

Forgiveness was at the heart of Jesus' teaching and ministry, because he knew that forgiveness was a restorative, healing event. Then, as now, many had to have their consciousness raised about the fact of sin in their lives—the disordered relationships that result, the close connection between sin and disease; the fact that wholeness is dependent on a restoration of our relationship with God, which restoration unclogs the spring of love and forgiveness so that it may flow from us to heal our broken relationships with others (*AC*, pp. 66–67).

Reflecting and Recording

There are two kinds of guilt in most of our lives: true guilt is what we feel when we are aware that we have done wrong or have failed to do something the Lord wishes us to do. False guilt is what we continue to feel after we've been forgiven for what we have done. True guilt moves us to repentance and the acceptance of God's forgiveness through Jesus Christ. False guilt clogs the channels of God's restorative, healing grace in our lives.

Examine your own life now. Are you feeling guilty? Check those feelings. Are they the result of something wrong or some hurtful thing you have done which you have not yet acknowledged or confessed? Stop now and think about it.

✳ ✳ ✳

Are your feelings *true guilt?* If so, are you repentant? Do you feel genuinely sorry and are you willing to make amends wherever possible? Confess to the Lord and receive forgiveness.

✳ ✳ ✳

Are your feelings *false guilt?* Have you already confessed and repented? If so, look beyond the assumed reason for your guilt. There may be reasons why you cannot accept forgiveness. If this inability to receive forgiveness persists, you may need to see a minister or a counselor. Maybe you simply do not yet believe that forgiveness is for you. Claim this promise. "If we confess our sins, he is faithful and just, and will forgive our sins and cleanse us from all unrighteousness" (1 John 1:9, RSV).

✳ ✳ ✳

During the Day

The indwelling Christ is a forgiving, healing presence. Memorize the above verse (1 John 1:9), and take it with you during the days ahead. When feelings of guilt emerge, quote that scripture to yourself and claim the freedom Christ offers.

Day Four: *The Connection between Forgiveness and Healing*

It was in another city, and I was preaching some special evangelistic services. I'd seen him at the service every day—in the morning and in the evening. He was a handsome young man. I was introduced to him, and I could tell by looking at him that something was going on in his life. His eyes were troubled and searching. Though handsome, there was a tightness about his face that betrayed a troubled spirit.

Finally he got the nerve to ask to see me. He came to my motel in the afternoon and began to share. He told me about his past life: sexual promiscuity; an abortion on the part of the one he loved, but to whom he was not yet married; their marriage; then their life together. They now had one child and were a happy family, but he was stricken with what we call a terminal illness. What was going on in this young man was tremendous guilt, guilt over his past sin, the failure of his life in so many ways. But now, added to his guilt, was that haunting feeling, that ravaging, tearing-apart feeling that his present illness was God's punishment for his past sins.

I shared the gospel as clearly as I could, talked about God's forgiving grace, about the love of Jesus and his call to repentance. The young man received the gospel, repented, and was reborn as clearly as anyone I know could be reborn. He went from our time together rejoicing. That was six months ago from the time of this writing, and that young man is in remission from his so-called terminal illness.

Now that's a dramatic story, and it doesn't always happen that way. But there are enough of these dramatic stories to keep getting our attention, and to keep reminding us that Jesus' call is to repentance and his offer is forgiveness and new birth, freedom from sin and wholeness of life. Forgiveness and healing go together.

Read the following story carefully.

When [Jesus] returned to Capernaum after some days, it was reported that he was at home. And many were gathered together, so that there was no longer room for them, not even about the door; and he was preaching the word to them. And they came, bringing to him a paralytic carried by four men. And when they could not get near him because of the crowd, they removed the roof above him; and when they had made an opening, they let down the pallet on which the paralytic lay. And when Jesus saw their faith, he said to the paralytic, "My son, your sins are forgiven." Now some of the scribes were sitting there, questioning in their hearts, "Why does this man speak thus? It is blasphemy! Who can forgive sins but God alone?" And immediately Jesus, perceiving in his spirit that they thus questioned within themselves, said to them,

"Why do you question thus in your hearts? Which is easier, to say to the paralytic, 'Your sins are forgiven?' or to say 'Rise, take up your pallet and walk'? But that you may know that the Son of man has authority on earth to forgive sins"—he said to the paralytic—"I say to you, rise, take up your pallet and go home." And he rose, and immediately took up the pallet and went out before them all; so that they were all amazed and glorified God, saying, "We never saw anything like this!"

—Mark 2:1–12, RSV

Do you see the intimate link between forgiveness and healing? The picture is at once pathetic and hopeful, tragic and heroic. The fellow is immobilized, but his friends are courageous and hopeful. They are so convinced of the power of Jesus to heal, and so bold in their pursuit of this healing that they knocked a hole in the ceiling of the house where Jesus was teaching in order to get the man to Jesus.

What happened then astounded those present as it may astound us if we give it thought. Jesus, seeing the faith of the man and the four fellows who brought him, announced to the paralytic, "My son, your sins are forgiven" (Mark 2:5). *What is going on here?* the men must have thought. *We didn't bring him here to have his sins absolved. Why, the poor fellow can't walk. We want him up and out of that stretcher.* They must have also been deeply puzzled, as were others in the crowd, and shocked at the blasphemy of such an announcement, "Who can forgive sins but God?" (v. 7).

The interesting fact is that no one doubted what was going on; the question had to do with who was doing it. Knowing that, Jesus completed his act of mercy and affirmed his self-awareness, making clear his mission. He healed the paralytic. Mark records that Jesus explained his reason for doing this. "Why must you argue like this in your minds? Which do you suppose is easier—to say to a paralysed man, 'Your sins are forgiven,' or 'Get up, pick up your bed and walk'? But to prove to you that the Son of Man has full authority to forgive sins on earth, I say to you,"—and here he spoke to the paralytic—"Get up, pick up your bed and go home" (vv. 8–11 Phillips).

The fellow sprang to his feet, picked up his bed and walked away, leaving no doubt about the power of Jesus to forgive and heal (*AC*, pp. 74–75).

Now, let's be clear. Sickness is not punishment for sin. There is a connection, however, between physical and spiritual disease. To put it more positively, there is an intimate link between our spiritual health and our physical and mental well-being. It is clear, not only from the scriptural story we are looking at today, but from Jesus' entire ministry that Jesus connected forgiveness and healing.

Reflecting and Recording

Examine some of your emotional patterns by briefly describing experiences of the following nature. Write enough to remember and get in touch with the experience.

1. Describe and experience when you were so upset that you could not eat.

2. When were you so angry that you could not sleep?

3. Describe a conflict with your spouse, or another loved one, which gave you such an excruciating headache or upset stomach that you had to get away from the relationship for a time to find relief.

Is there enough evidence in these simple experiences to show the connection between physical and emotional disease?

Look at each of those experiences and see if there was a specific connection between your physical dis-ease and unrelieved guilt, unconfessed, or unforgiven sin.

✳   ✳   ✳

During the Day

Tomorrow we will continue thinking about this connection between spiritual/emotional/physical dis-ease.

During the day be sensitive to the signals you receive from your body when things are not going well emotionally or spiritually.

Day Five: *Some Spiritual Laws for Healing*

Dr. Hans Selye, a medical doctor in Montreal, Canada, has done extensive research on stress. Though his investigations were primarily in the science of biochemistry, he discovered that positive emotions and attitudes such as gratitude, thanksgiving, praise, forgiveness and joy, are health-enhancing factors. Likewise, negative emotions and attitudes such as resentment, anger, hate, and jealousy, have a debilitating and disease-inducing effect on the body. (*See The Stress of Life* and *Stress without Distress*).

In a recent weekend retreat in which I served as spiritual director, I counseled with a young woman who was suffering from rheumatoid arthritis. She wore a back brace for a part of each day, and her pain was so intense that she would slip away from the group at break time to suffer alone.

She also had other physical problems about which she hesitantly shared. I had not known her before and learned of her suffering from some women who were a part of her small table group in the conference.

Late on the second day of the weekend, I told her I knew of her health situation, and I asked about her feelings. By a miracle of the Spirit, which often happens when we genuinely care and are willing to listen, a *meeting* happened. Soul touched soul in genuine dialogue, and she began to share deeply. Usually much more time is required; but grace was working in "high gear," and within ten minutes she shared a malignant resentment and unresolved guilt that was poisoning her whole being.

She was very active in her church as a young person, played the piano for worship and was involved in the youth program. When she was eighteen, the summer before she went to college, she was practicing her music at the church. The new pastor of the congregation made sexual advances and propositioned her. The church had just gone through a struggle which centered around the previous pastor and tore the congregation apart. Her father was a deacon of the church and on the pulpit committee which had asked for the previous pastor's resignation and had played a large role in engaging the new pastor for the church.

My friend felt trapped. There was no one with whom to share her disillusionment and hurt, lest the congregation be completely splintered and her father's leadership be discredited. Her disillusionment and hurt became resentment and bitterness. As the resentment and bitterness seethed within, it closed her off from free participation in the Christian community and cultivated an almost paranoid distrust of ministers.

The church she attends now often has prayer times when the minister invites persons to come to the altar for prayer—to pray with him if they desire. "I've longed to do that on so many occasions," she said, "but I couldn't force myself to kneel with a preacher." That's the awful degree to which her bitter distrust had grown.

I cautiously laid my hand on her shoulder as I kept eye contact to communicate acceptance and love. (I felt a touch from a pastor was essential for her beginning healing.) She literally shuddered when I touched her, though she didn't withdraw. In a few sentences, with all the caring I could communicate, I told her that she was allowing that experience of the past to rob her of the love and joy Christ was offering. Our conversation ended as she admitted her awareness of this and painfully confessed that she had been unable to do anything about it.

During the retreat there was a special communion service, in which persons broke a piece of bread from a common loaf and named some experience of the past, some shattered relationship, or some personal problem or habit to which they wished to die. They later received these pieces of broken bread, along with the cup, as the body and blood of Christ in Holy Communion. My friend named her experience with the pastor as her dying moment.

The next day, as the weekend was closing, her small group leader, at my friend's request, asked me to share with them in the chapel. She was being moved to make a deeper commitment to Christ.

The Spirit led me to say to her that the big barrier to assurance of her salvation and to her spiritual wholeness at that time was the fact that she had not forgiven the preacher who had sinned against her. Though he had not asked her forgiveness, she must forgive him.

To make explicit her commitment, I did what I often find helpful. I asked her to repeat after me a prayer that would become her own. She was more than willing. The group leader who was with us did not know the story of her bitterness and resentment, so I worded the prayer in a way that would be understood by my friend but would not violate her confidence.

"Lord, I forgive the one who hurt me so deeply fifteen years ago."

There was silence. She couldn't say it. I repeated it. "Lord, I forgive...''; more silence, but now she was breathing hard and her body was shaking. I placed my arm around her shoulders in a partial embrace and remained quiet as her body gradually relaxed. Again I said, "Lord, I forgive..."

Then it came—her own prayer. "Lord, I forgive the one who hurt me so deeply fifteen years ago." Her body relaxed more, and she continued the prayer of commitment in confidence and with strength in her quivering voice.

This happened three weeks ago from this writing. Last week my friend drove a great distance to be with her group leader and another woman from the conference. She shared her whole story with her friends, telling them the release she has experienced, the relief from her arthritic pain, the joyous assurance of being accepted by the Lord, and the meaningful experience she is having in prayer.

James K. Wagner, in his book *Blessed to Be a Blessing,* called my attention to Dr. Loring T. Swaim, a physician. Dr. Swaim specialized for fifty years in the field of orthopedics, and for twenty years was an instructor in arthritis at Harvard Medical School. He published a significant study in 1962 (*Arthritis, Medicine, and the Spiritual Laws,* New York: Chilton Company).

The book is filled with well-documented, matter-of-fact case histories of his patients. Dr. Swaim describes what can happen when ordinary persons "tangled in the intricate web of human nature and crippled by disease, are set free by the surrender of resentment and bitterness and the submission of self-will to God."

Dr. Swaim, along with a growing number of medical doctors, is convinced that emotional stress such as negative attitudes toward others can be causative of rheumatoid arthritis and other organic diseases. If not causative, then negative attitudes certainly weaken our resistance and make us more vulnerable to organic disease.

Again, no one would say that what any one of us is suffering from is caused in this fashion, but the data dictates that we examine ourselves daily to see if we are not allowing ourselves to come under stress, or make ourselves vulnerable to physical disease by failing to appropriate the forgiving and healing power of the indwelling Christ.

Reflecting and Recording

Along with treating his patients with the latest medical and physical therapies, Dr. Swaim prescribed spiritual therapy for those who were receptive and willing. He offers five spiritual laws which lead to improved health and wholeness.

The Law of Love: "This is my commandment, that you love one another as I have loved you. Greater love has no man than this, that a man lay down his life for his friends" (John 15:12–13, RSV).

The Law of Apology: "So if you are offering your gift at the altar, and there remember that your brother has something against you, leave your gift there before the altar and go; first be reconciled to your brother, and then come and offer your gift" (Matt. 5:23–24, RSV).

The Law of Change: "You hypocrite, first take the log out of your own eye, and then you will see clearly to take the speck out of your brother's eye" (Matt. 7:5, RSV).

The Law Concerning Fault-Finding: "Judge not, that you be not judged" (Matt. 7:1, RSV); "So whatever you wish that men would do to you, do so to them; for this is the law and the prophets" (Matt. 7:12, RSV).

The Law of Forgiveness: "For if you forgive men their trespasses, your heavenly Father also will forgive you; but if you do not forgive men their trespasses, neither will your Father forgive your trespasses" (Matt. 6:14, RSV).

Look at your life. Are there things going on now or past experiences to which you need to apply these spiritual laws? Reflective self-examination is important and may reveal some hidden source of discomfort, dis-ease, or some block to wholeness. Spend some time in this process.

✳   ✳   ✳

During the Day

Which "law" will you specifically put into practice today?

Day Six: *Inner Healing*

Yesterday, I mentioned the "dying moment" model of Holy Communion. This sharing always provides one of the most powerful experiences of grace I know. It is a dramatic expression of the death and resurrection motif of the Christian life. As we saw in Week Two, that motif was dominant in Paul's teaching—dying and rising with Christ.

You have died, and your life is hid with Christ in God.
—Colossians 3:3, RSV

You were buried with [Christ] in baptism, in which you were also raised with him through faith in the working of God, who raised him from the dead.
—Colossians 2:12, RSV

If we have died with Christ, we believe that we shall also live with him.
—Romans 6:8, RSV

In a "dying moment" on a recent retreat, three women shared the need to die to the painful memory of having been sexually molested during their pre-adolescence. For two of these, it was a healing experience to confess that painful memory and to receive the vivid expression of love and grace in the bread and wine, the body and blood of Christ.

For the third (let's call her Mary), that was not enough. The pain, resentment, and hatred had grown in her memory and was like a fire burning in her being. An irrational shame about sex hindered a meaningful sexual relation with her husband, and threatened her marriage. She felt she was harboring a dark secret that could never be shared, and the burden of that weighed her down.

Mary sought out my clergy friend who was sharing spiritual leadership that weekend. Sensitively, with gentle but probing love, Rick counseled with her, then led her in a "healing of memories." At his prompting and guidance, she went back to the experience in her memory, relived the fear, pain, helplessness, and shame of it, inviting Christ to be present with her through that trying time, and to heal her of all the distress and emotional trauma of that experience.

Rick asked Mary to receive from Christ a sign of his healing, and to share with him the sign Christ offered. After the experience she told Rick that in her imagination, Christ had placed a cross around her neck, and told her that when she wore the cross or saw another cross, to remember her healing.

That gift of Christ in imagination was powerfully underscored as the weekend retreat closed. Mary, who received that gift from Christ, did not know that the next day she would be given a cross in a closing time of dedication, and that the spiritual director would place that cross around her neck and remind her that "Christ was counting on her." The community did not realize the ecstatic joy that brought for Mary. It was the final confirmation she needed for her inner healing.

The indwelling Christ as a forgiving/healing presence wants to walk back into the dark places of our lives, live with us our memory at those distressing and painful intersections, and touch us with love saying "your sins are forgiven, your faith has saved you, go in peace." If we believe as Christians that our Lord Christ is not limited by time and space, that he is the same today as he was yesterday and will be forever (Heb. 13:8), then his healing is not limited to the present. He can go back in time and be as vitally alive in our memories (which are often as real to us as this morning's experience) as he is real to us in our prayers to him this day.

Healing the past, our memories, negative emotions, all come under the rubric of *inner healing,* and so our healing can be complete in Christ.

Reflecting and Recording

Assuming that you may have a need for inner healing, here is a guide for you to follow in claiming that healing. It may be that you will want to share with a minister or a trusted spiritual friend this need in your life and invite their assistance.

Get in a comfortable place where you can be quiet and relax. Use some relaxing exercises if necessary to release the tensions in your body. Free your mind and begin to move back in your memory to the painful experience and/or relationships.

Affirm the fact that Christ is with you. He is present. It may be helpful to acknowledge that or to extend a specific invitation. "Christ, I'm about to experience in my mind something very painful and distressing to me. I need and want you to be with me. Walk back with me now in my memory."

Visualize the place.... (This takes a bit of time, but concretizing reality is important.)

Get a picture of the persons involved.... Can you recall any conversation? Specific words? It will be painful now, but this is essential. Feel the sting of the words.... the physical pain.... the emotional strain.... the fear.... the helplessness.... the burden of bearing your "secret" alone....

Re-experiencing the feelings are as important as getting in touch with the details, so take your time to relive your memory.

Do you need to do something? To speak to someone? Do you need to tell someone who is in the experience the pain they caused you, the shame, or guilt? Do you need to ask their forgiveness for what you did to them, or offer yours for what they did to you?

Christ is with you. Remember that. He has been with you in this total experience. Talk to him now, and let him talk to you. Listen to what he says.

Let him touch you if he wishes. Above all, concentrate on his eyes and see the compassion and care he has for you. Know that he is saying, "Be healed, your faith has saved you, your sins are forgiven."

Would you like to offer Christ a gift? Or receive one from him— some sign or seal of your healing to take with you from this place? Maybe just a word that you will remember forever.

Don't leave the experience of memory now until you claim Christ's healing. He offers it; we must receive it.

During the Day

The goal of inner healing is to be set free, to be released from some painful past experience and to live joyfully in the present without fear of the future. It will help you strengthen your inner healing by sharing it with another. Do that sometime today as you are able.

Day Seven: *Physical Healing*

There are four kinds of healing: spiritual, emotional, physical and relational. We need to think of healing in its broadest sense, the healing presence of the indwelling Christ ministering to our *total* situation.

So the healing presence is not always the dramatic healing of physical or mental disorder to which we can give witness, though sometimes it is. And the healing is not always instantaneous and complete, though there has been such. Most often, healing is a process. The indwelling Christ moves into an area of our life which we open to him, to provide transformation and healing. Not only physically, but perhaps in even more important ways, Christ heals. To the degree of our willingness and openness and yieldedness, we are healed of bitterness, hatred, painful memories, wounded spirits, sores of the soul kept open and infected by estrangement from loved ones, the ravaging grief of a broken heart because of the death of a loved one, the despondency that has come from vocational failure, the frozen will that has come from defeat. (*AC,* pp. 78–79).

But we can't ignore the specifically physical. Because we are unable to make any connections between the emotional/spiritual and the physical, or because we may not have the time or skill to probe for reasons, does not mean that we should not seek the physical healing Jesus surely offers.

Do we need a story?

Now there is in Jerusalem by the Sheep Gate a pool, in Hebrew called Bethzatha, which has five porticoes. In these lay a multitude of invalids, blind, lame, paralyzed. One man was there, who had been ill for thirty-eight years. When Jesus saw him and knew that he had been lying there a long time, he said to him, "Do you want to be healed?" The sick man answered him, "Sir, I have no man to put me into the pool when the water is troubled, and while I am going another steps down before me." Jesus said to him, "Rise, take up your pallet, and walk." And at once the man was healed, and he took up his pallet and walked.

—John 5:2–9, RSV

The story is rich in meaning and challenging in the questions it raises.

Jesus asked the man if he wanted to be healed. *We play a role in our healing;* we have to be willing. Did the man enjoy being sick? Some people do. Sickness brings attention, gives us some measure of control over others, frees us of certain responsibilities.

Jesus knew all this, and he questioned the man. But the bottom line was that the fellow was physically healed. He took up his pallet and walked.

Physical healing is an important and complex subject, and I regret that I cannot consider it in more depth here. We can't look at the healing presence of the indwelling Christ without acknowledging the physical aspect specifically. At the end of this section, I have listed a few books, I recommend for those who wish to pursue this matter.

For now, this perspective is helpful. Danny Morris, in his book, *Any Miracle God Wants to Give,* shares some learnings from Dr. J. C. McPheeters who believed that there are five miracles of healing which God gives.

The instant cure—Though rare, they do occur and have been witnessed to.

God's undertaking—God has created us with the natural capacity to be healed. When these operate, God is *undertaking* our healing.

God's guidance to a remedy—Oftentimes we are directed to the right doctor, the right prescription, the right relationship to bring healing—choosing a doctor or a hospital should be a matter of prayer, for it is a part of God's healing ministry to guide us to a remedy for our sickness.

The sufficiency of God's grace—The classic example is Paul's overcoming of his "thorn in the flesh." He prayed for deliverance, but did not receive it. Yet, the Lord said to him, "My grace is sufficient for you," and Paul lived victoriously in spite of his suffering.

The triumphant crossing—This is the healing of the resurrection, and the ultimate healing. Death is inevitable. No matter how many healings we may experience, one day we will die. It is a central certainty of the Christian faith that the sting of death has been pulled, death no longer has ultimate power over us, for God has raised Jesus from the dead and given us the gift of eternal life.

In recent months in our church, we have prayed for Ed, a man with a brain tumor. He has taken all the regular chemotherapy and cobalt treatments, and has been cared for by excellent doctors who say the tumor has been reduced. We feel we have participated in his healing. We have also prayed for Mary, who has a malignancy in her liver. She has not been healed, though we have prayed in the same fashion as we prayed for Ed, and she has also received excellent medical care.

So, we live with the mystery—claiming Christ's healing power, yet continuing to trust him when death tests our faith in Christ's healing presence. We accept any miracle he would give, but also live with suffering and death, knowing that he will use that also.

To be alive in Christ is to be alive in the world, bearing its sin, its shame, its grief, and its agony. The indwelling Christ is a healing presence, even in the midst of sin, shame, grief, and agony. In him we know what we are doing and what the outcome will be, for his resurrection is our daily hope and glory (*AC,* p. 80).

Reflecting and Recording

John H. Parke, past warden of the Order of St. Luke the Physician, a fellowship of Christians dedicated to recovering the healing ministry of the church, has given us a way to pray for our own healing. You may use this as a guide and also adapt it in praying for others.

1. **Realize**
   Know that you were born for a glorious, triumphant, and whole life, that the will of God for you is good, that the Great Physician wills wholeness for you.

2. **Repent**
   Not all illness is caused by sin, but usually somewhere, somehow, a physical or moral law of the universe has been broken, willfully or accidentally, either by you or by someone closely affecting your life. Insofar as you may have been at fault, confession and a sincere desire to change is needed. Where another may be responsible, your forgiveness of that person is required (Mark 11:25–26; James 5:16). Put away all hostility toward conditions, circumstances, persons, places and things.

3. **Relax**
   Consciously release all the tensions of your body, all the doubts and anxieties of your mind. Lay aside all criticism, prejudices, and preconceived notions, and keep an open mind. Let go and let God.

4. **Visualize Perfect Health**
   Reverse the negative patterns of disease, limitation, and troubles. Do not publicize your ills and complaints. Using your imagination, see yourself the way you believed God wants you to be—perfect wholeness in every part of your being—body, mind and spirit. Visualize Jesus, the Great Physician, reaching forward to touch you. As you feel his touch, know that his healing power is flowing within you.

5. **Ask**
   And you shall receive (Matthew 7:7). "Whatsoever ye shall ask in my name, that will I do" (John 14:13). Ask with faith—"Lord, I believe" (Mark 9:24). "Believe that you have received it, and it will be yours" (Mark 11:24) Ask with thanksgiving—"Father, I thank thee that thou hast heard me" (John 11:41). Even before any results

are evident, start thanking God that his healing power is at work. Say with joy—"Jesus, I praise you. Jesus, I love you"—just pour our your heart in praise and love to him.

6. Accept

Let God touch every area of your life with his power. Realize God's presence continually. Live in the now, think in the now, and act in the now. Live in a constant state of expectancy of God's constant adequacy.

7. Do Something in Response to Your Healing

Do something that you could not do before. Do something for someone else who needs you. Do something special for God. Witness to all what God has done for you. (Parke, pp. 16–17).

During the Day

As suggested above, do something in response to your healing today.

Additional Reading

Bonnell, John Sutherland; *Do You Want To Be Healed?* New York: Harper & Rowe Publishers, 1968.

Day, Albert E. *Letters on the Healing Ministry.* Nashville: The Upper Room, 1986.

MacNutt, Francis *Healing* Notre Dame, IN: Ave Maria, 1974.

Morris, Danny E. *Any Miracle God Wants to Give.* Nashville: The Upper Room, 1974.

Stranger, Frank B. *God's Healing Community.* Nashville: Abingdon, 1978.

Wagner, James K. *Blessed to Be A Blessing.* Nashville: The Upper Room, 1980.

Group Meeting for Week Four

Introduction

Paul advised the Philippians to ''let your conversation be as it becometh the gospel'' (Phil. 1:27, KJV). Most of us have yet to see the dynamic potential of the conversation which takes place in an intentional group such as this. The Elizabethan word for *life* as used in the King James version is *conversation,* thus Paul's word to the Philippians. Life is found in communion with God and also in conversation with others.

Speaking and listening with this sort of deep meaning which communicates life is not easy. This week our emphasis has been on forgiving and healing, deep experiences not easy to talk about. Therefore, listening and responding to what we hear is very important. To really hear another person may contribute to the healing process. To listen, then, is an act of love. When we listen in a way that makes a difference, we surrender ourselves to the other person, saying, ''I will hear what you have to say and will receive you as I receive your words.'' When we speak in a way that makes a difference, we speak for the sake of others, thus we are contributing to the wholeness process.

Sharing Together

1. Begin your sharing with a ten-to-fifteen-minute discussion on why people do not receive forgiveness. Urge persons to make this personal by referring to their notes on Day Two of this week.

2. Move from this into a discussion of *true* and *false* guilt. Again, be personal by sharing actual experiences of true and false guilt.

3. On Day Four, we considered the link between forgiveness and healing, between physical and emotional dis-ease. Invite two or three persons to share experiences recorded on that day, i.e., so upset they could not eat, so angry they couldn't sleep, a conflict with a spouse or loved one that brought some physical illness. If the sharer is willing, ask him or her to share whether there was a connection between the physical dis-ease and unrelieved guilt—unconfessed or unforgiven sin.

4. On Day Seven we considered five miracles of healing which God gives. Spend a bit of time talking about these, sharing new insights and questions that may have arisen.

5. On days Five and Six, I shared two stories about physical and emotional (inner) healing. This is a very sensitive area and not easy to talk about. Remind the group of this, so that no pressure will be felt. But ask the group if anyone wishes to share an experience of this nature that may be meaningful, informing, and enriching. Remember, it doesn't have to be *dramatic*. Sometimes that which looks insignificant, even superficial, can be a barrier to wholeness. To be freed from any experience, however minor in appearance, that blocks our joyful life in Christ is worth celebrating.

Praying Together

Corporate prayer is one of the great blessings of Christian community. To affirm that is one thing; to experience it is another. To *experience* it we have to *experiment* with the possibility. Will you become a bit bolder now, and experiment with the possibilities of corporate prayer by sharing more openly and intimately?

1. Spend three to five minutes in quietness now, asking and answering these two questions. Is there a specific need for forgiveness in my life? Do I have a need for physical, emotional, or spiritual healing?

2. Let each person who will share one need for forgiveness and/or healing. As this is done, other persons in the group may find it helpful to take notes on this sharing, so you can pray in a more centered way.

3. There is a sense in which, through this sharing, you have already been corporately praying. There is power, however, in a community on a common journey verbalizing thoughts and feelings to God in the presence of fellow pilgrims. Experiment with this possibility now.

A. Let the leader call each person's name, pausing briefly after each name for some person in the group to offer a brief verbal prayer focused on what that person has shared. It should be as simple as, ''Lord, give Jane the confidence that she is forgiven,'' or ''Loving God, give John the sense of your healing power in his struggle with _____.''
(Leader, remember to call your own name.)

B. When all names have been called and all persons prayed for, sit in silence for two minutes; be open to the strength of love that is ours in community. *Enjoy* being linked with persons who are mutually concerned.

4. If it seems appropriate, close this prayer time with the leader, or someone designated by the leader beforehand, leading the group in the prayer process for healing, steps one through five, on p. 105. The person doing this should have people sit comfortably with eyes closed, then simply read the steps slowly, giving time of silence after each to allow persons to actually do what they are being called to do.

If this process is used, then after prayer time, remind group of steps six and seven.

Close by simply saying, "Amen."

A Guiding and Creating Presence

Day One: *Led by the Spirit as Children of God*

There is a marvelous word in Romans 8:14 which is the foundation of our theme this week: The indwelling Christ as a guiding and creating presence. Savor that word: "For all who are led by the Spirit of God are sons of God" (RSV).

Throughout the New Testament, especially in the writings of John and Paul, the Holy Spirit, the Spirit of God and the Spirit of Christ are used interchangeably and are often indistinguishable. Paul's word quoted above follows a passage in which it is impossible to distinguish Christ dwelling within from the Holy Spirit. Consider that passage.

> You are on the spiritual level, if only God's Spirit dwells within you; and if a man does not possess the Spirit of Christ, he is no Christian. But if Christ is dwelling within you, then although the body is a dead thing because you sinned, yet the spirit is life itself because you have been justified. Moreover, if the Spirit of him who raised Jesus from the dead dwells within you, then the God who raised Christ Jesus from the dead will also give new life to your mortal bodies through his indwelling Spirit.
>
> —Romans 8:9–11, NEB

In John 14:18 Jesus says: "I will not leave you desolate; I will come to you" (RSV). He then makes it clear that his Spirit, the Spirit of God, will be an abiding presence in their lives.

This week we concentrate on this presence as *guiding* and *creating*. "For all who are led by the Spirit of God are sons of God."

111

The indwelling Christ is a guiding presence. Any one of us can call from our memory occasions when we knew for certain that we were being guided. But how much of the time do we live in anxiety, uncertain about the direction in which we should go, immobilized by choices, impotent in the presence of opportunity because we are indecisive? We need guidance and we can't lay hold of it.

There are great decisions in life—vocation, marriage, career movement, crisis situations—when our need for guidance is vividly pronounced. But what plagues us most and drains us of so much energy are the intersections upon which we come every day, when we have to choose which way to go. To be sure, we need guidance at the major intersections of our lives, but we need it also at the little crossings and turnings of which our lives primarily consist. My plea is that we see guidance not as episodic, but as an ongoing dynamic which shapes our beings and thus determines decisions and directions.

The guidance of the indwelling Christ is consistent and ongoing. This does not mean that there are not specific times when we seek explicit guidance in particular situations. It does mean that through prayer and other spiritual disciplines we seek to cultivate the awareness of the indwelling Christ to the point that we are delivered from a frantic disposition of mind and heart in the face of decision. We do not come "cold turkey" to a minor or a major crisis. We have the inner sense of Christ's presence. Calling upon that presence, direction is often so clear that the right decision does not even require deciding (*AC,* p. 84).

Reflecting and Recording

In your mind, walk through the waking time of your past twenty-four hours. In the following time frames make some notes that will assure that you have looked carefully at your day. Pay attention to persons you were with, decisions you had to make, things you had to do. Don't write in the column to the right yet.

EXAMINATION OF AN ORDINARY DAY

6:00 A.M.–9:00 A.M.

9:00 A.M.–11:00 A.M.

11:00 A.M.–2:00 P.M.

2:00 P.M.–5:00 P.M.

5:00 P.M.–8:00 P.M.

8:00 P.M.–Midnight

Now, in your mind walk again through your day, but first read the questions below. In the space to the right, make notes about each time period in response to these questions.

Did I need *special* guidance in that situation, relationship, or task?
Did I seek guidance?
Did I feel guidance even though I didn't specifically seek it?
Did I pray in any of these time frames? For what did I pray?
Did any scripture come to my mind?

Go back now and make your notes.

* * *

What does this examination of an ordinary day say about your need for and your experiencing the guiding presence of the indwelling Christ?

* * *

During the Day

Having examined the waking hours of your preceeding day, move through the day ahead alert to your need for, and experience of, the indwelling Christ as a guiding presence.

Day Two: *A Personal Experience*

At the time of the most difficult professional decision of my life, the following scripture came alive in my life. "I will not leave you desolate; I will come to you. Yet a little while, and the world will see me no more, but you will see me; because I live, you will live also. In that day you will know that I am in my Father, and you in me, and I in you" (John 14:18–20, RSV).

I was the World Editor of The Upper Room engaged in the most exciting and challenging ministry of my life. I had no notion of leaving, though I had told my bishop that someday I wanted to be a pastor again. Deep down I knew that was my primary calling.

It happened abruptly and shockingly. Ed Tullis, not only my bishop but a trusted friend, called me in the middle of the night from a distant city saying he wanted to see me when he returned to Nashville the next evening; he wanted to talk to me about going to be the Senior Minister at Christ Church, Memphis.

A few weeks earlier, another bishop had offered the possibility for me to be the pastor of one of the largest churches in Methodism. It took me about ten minutes to make a decision in response to that offer. But this was *my* bishop talking, and I knew I had to hear him out.

His conversation with my wife Jerry and me led to an interview with the Staff-Parish Committee of Christ Church and their invitation to be their pastor. I wrestled with the issue for about two weeks. Then came the January weekend in 1982 in Nashville when we were almost snowbound. Sunday morning my car wouldn't start, so I couldn't go to church.

Normally I wouldn't say that it is providential for one to stay home from church. But that Sunday it was.

Jerry and I spent most of that Sunday sitting by the fire. We had ceased *wrestling* and had relinquished the situation to God, having come to the place where we were willing to act upon whatever guidance we received. So the day was a quiet one of *resting;* I believe, "resting in the Lord." We would struggle no longer. We would simply do as best we could what the scripture calls us to do: "Wait on the Lord." The word of Jesus resounded in my mind, "In that day, you will know that I am in the Father, and you in me, and I in you."

No clarity came—no distinct guidance, but we went to bed that night believing that, somehow, direction would come. The next morning I awoke with the conviction that I should call the Staff-Parish chairperson, believing that one more visit with the committee would confirm the feeling that was emerging within that I should accept this appointment. That happened, and at the close of the meeting, I told the church I would come to be their pastor.

I share this experience to affirm my conviction about the guiding presence of the indwelling Christ and to give a sequel to the story. I had only one deep grief occasion during the transition from The Upper Room back to the pastorate.

About four months after I went to Memphis, at the close of two deeply meaningful retreats I was leading in Virginia, as I left the closing service to pick up my suitcase and head for the airport, I was overcome with sadness. Tears came freely. It hit me hard. This was the kind of ministry that had been the normal pattern of my life, and was a carry-over from my former ministry at The Upper Room. While I would be doing some of that in the future, it would be the exception rather than the norm.

That sadness stayed with me for about an hour. But here is the miracle. I was returning to Memphis through Nashville, stopping there for a two-day meeting at The Upper Room—my first return since leaving. As I landed in Nashville, I had a strange feeling. I knew I wasn't at *home;* I was *visiting*. I would do my work and then head home to Memphis where I belonged. It was a work of grace in my heart. It was a sort of finishing confirmation about the rightness of the Lord's leading, and I knew, without doubt, that the graceful guiding presence was that of the indwelling Christ.

The word that had come to me as I sat by the fire that Sunday, when I was "waiting" on the Lord, was underlined in my life. "In that day you will know that I am in my Father, and you in me, and I in you."

Reflecting and Recording

Yesterday you were asked to look at your life in terms of ongoing guidance. You were also asked to move through the day alert to your need for and experience of the indwelling Christ as a guiding presence. Did your day hold any such experiences? If so, make some notes about them here.

Now, apart from ongoing guidance, search back and locate the most recent experience when you felt *definitely* guided. It doesn't have to be as pivotal and dramatic as the one I shared above, but get in touch with such an experience. Write enough about it to get in touch with and, perhaps, relive the experience.

During the Day

Memorize this word of Jesus: "In that day, you will know that I am in my Father, and you in me, and I in you" (John 14:20, RSV).

✳ ✳ ✳

That day Jesus is talking about is *now*. He was pointing forward to his death and his resurrection; his being freed from the flesh in order to be a constant presence with us.

Repeat the promise of Jesus again and again this day; especially remind yourself of it when you have to make a choice or a decision. Believe that Christ is *in you* as a guiding presence.

Day Three: *The Guiding Presence in Prayer*

In Weeks One and Two, we concentrated on an understanding of the indwelling Christ. We defined spiritual formation in terms of *recognizing and exercising* the indwelling Christ. One big aspect of prayer, then, is *recognizing* and *cultivating an awareness* of the indwelling Christ.

Christian prayer is characteristically a way of seeking to bring our wills into harmony with God's will. Yet, prayer is often distorted, even by Christians, as an effort to bring God's power to bear upon the accomplishment of our will. We decide what is right and good, then we beseech God to bring it about, or at least help us accomplish it. Though the difference between these two approaches may seem subtle in theory, in practice they are often glaringly at odds. In Christian prayer we seek to orient ourselves to the divine picture of the world. We seek God's perspective—to see ourselves, our problems, our possibilities, our suffering, our dreams through the eyes of Christ.

It is precisely at this point that we must distinguish Christian spirituality from other forms of spirituality. John Cobb makes this point clearly as he calls for our spirituality to be more inherently and essentially integrated with the concern about what is happening in the world, rather than becoming privatistic. I quote him extensively because he makes the point so well.

Taking prayer as the center of what's often thought of as spirituality, we have to ask what is the distinctive character of Christian prayer. I assume the Lord's Prayer is as normative for understanding Christian prayer as anything could be. We ask ourselves the question, "What is really going on if we genuinely pray, 'Thy kingdom come, thy will be done.' " That is a very political prayer. The function of the prayer is that through praying it we come to orient ourselves toward what we are praying for.

I'm interested in oriental religions. I think the influence of oriental notions of spirituality has cut in the opposite direction of what I advance authentic Christian spirituality to be. It's not that it's impractical, if I can take zen as an example. Zen enables one to perform whatever functions come one's way better than one could without the discipline of zen. It's eminently practical, but doesn't introduce any distinctive judgement upon which practices are the appropriate ones. A pianist can play the piano better and a samurai can be a better swordsman through the practice of zen. Zen is not a way of deciding whether or not one should be a swordsman or a pianist. That's quite different from biblical spirituality, where the primary focus seems to be upon aligning one's will with the will of God. Presumably God's will is not primarily directed to the excellence with which I perform my daily round. I don't mean to exclude that, but it isn't what I get from the Old and New Testaments as the primary focus. . . .

I don't think we understand the will of God properly in terms of any set of rules. That would be law rather than spirit. My translation of aligning my will with God's will is a transformation of point of view, to see the world or to think of the world more as God sees it and thinks of it. With respect to all the decisions of life, instead of asking the question if I can afford something, I'm asking whether God favors it, but that's also whether the world can afford it. I don't read the newspapers and ask how beneficial certain developments are for my class, my race, my nation, whatever, but rather how this is affecting life on this planet in the most comprehensive sense. (*Haelan,* Spring 1981)

The transformation of a point of view which Dr. Cobb says is at the heart of prayer—"aligning my will with God's"—for me as a Christian is accomplished by the indwelling Christ. The more vivid my awareness of this presence, the more clearly I understand the nature and character of this presence, the more confidently can I experience guidance, and the more certain I can be that my life is being aligned with God's will (*AC,* pp. 84–86).

Reflecting and Recording

Go back to the experience of guidance you wrote about during this period of reflecting and recording yesterday. What role, if any, did prayer play in that experience?

✳   ✳   ✳

Was there in your praying or in seeking guidance an effort to bring God's power to bear upon the accomplishment of your will, rather than an effort to align your will with God's?

✳   ✳   ✳

Can you recall an experience of the past few months when you sought to see yourself, your problems, your sufferings, your dreams, through the eyes of Christ? Make some notes about that experience here.

During the Day

Look ahead to the next twenty-four hours. According to what you know now, what situations, meetings, relationships, decisions, encounters are coming which you may need to look at through the eyes of Christ? List those here and on the next page.

1.

2.

3.

4.

Prayerfully commit them now to Christ. Decide that you will seek to see them through his eyes, and exercise his presence in the midst of them.

Day Four: *Struggle as a Part of Prayer and Guidance*

How many times have you sought guidance in prayer only to experience a despairing silence, an empty void within—no response from God, no certainty of direction? What happens then?

Sometimes we *panic* because we feel so alone and without hope.

Sometimes we *pretend* that we are led, that guidance *is* ours, so we muster all our energy to display outward confidence when inside our stomachs are convulsing with uncertainty.

Or—and this is the most common pattern—we pray, but we sense no guidance, we register no response from God, so we go quiet within.

What happens then—when we go quiet within? Usually we vacillate between two big feelings. The first big feeling is that *something is wrong with me*. I'm not good enough for God to respond to. Or, I guess my faith is too weak. Or, I simply don't know how to pray.

You've been there, haven't you? *I have*. And that's what bothers me about over-confident Christians. Nothing is more depressing for a person struggling in prayer, seeking guidance, than for another Christian to pretend that guidance is simple, easy to come by. You don't help another by projecting a Christian lifestyle that confesses only the victories, only the triumphs, only the certainties, without recognition and confession of the struggles, the doubts, the wrestlings. The people of God in scripture never witnessed to such snap-of-the-finger results from prayer. Listen to the psalmist:

God, do not keep silent;
do not be still, do not be quiet!
—Psalm 83:1, TEV

Will the Lord always reject us?
Will he never again be pleased with us?
Has he stopped loving us?
Does his promise no longer stand?
Has God forgotten to be merciful?
Has anger taken the place of his compassion?
—Psalm 77:7–9, TEV

Now listen to the psalmist as he climaxes that dirge: "What hurts me most is this—that God is no longer powerful" (Psalm 77:10, TEV).

What do we learn from the psalmist? *Struggle is a part of what prayer is all about.* To pretend to yourself or to another that you can get to the promised land without going through the wilderness is spiritual deception, and sooner or later such a house of clay will crumble around you.

A second big feeling which comes when we go quiet within because we sense no guidance and register no response from God in prayer is the gnawing, devastating suspicion that *prayer is meaningless*—that people claim far more about its power and effectiveness than they actually experience. That's what the psalmist was saying: "what hurts me most is this, that God is no longer powerful."

Do you shudder at the thought? I do. But, that's okay. To confess and express feelings like that is not sacrilege. It is the kind of honesty necessary for prayer to become that authentic struggle of a person seeking to bring his or her life under the lordship of Christ.

Reflecting and Recording

Write a couple of sentences about your own experiences with these feelings.

1. You feel that something is wrong with you because God doesn't seem to be responding to you and your prayers.

2. You suspect that people claim far more about the power and effectiveness of prayer than they actually experience.

If some person with whom you were sharing said either of the above things about prayer, what could you tell them from your own experience that would be helpful? Spend some time thinking about this.

※ ※ ※

During the Day

Again, today, do what I asked you to do yesterday. Look ahead to the next twenty-four hours. According to what you know now, what situations, meetings, relationships, decisions, or encounters are coming which you may need to look at through the eyes of Christ? List those here:

1.

2.

3.

4.

Prayerfully commit them now to Christ. Decide that you will seek to see them through his eyes, and exercise his presence in the midst of them.

Day Five: *Guidance through Scripture and Persons*

For the past two days, you were asked to look at your day and anticipate encounters, situations, decisions and relationships at which you needed to look through the eyes of Christ. Have you been doing that? Note here a couple of experiences that have resulted from that effort.

❋ ❋ ❋

Søren Kierkegaard suggested that "the bible should be read as a letter from God with our personal address on it." Scripture and prayer go together as a source of cultivating awareness of the indwelling Christ and availing ourselves to his guiding presence.

Of course scripture is a guide in a general way. Paul reminded Timothy that "all scripture is inspired by God and profitable for teaching, for reproof, for correction, and for training in righteousness, that the man of God may be complete, equipped for every good work" (2 Tim. 3:16–17, RSV). Scripture is a primary source of guidance for life. We need to see and use scripture specifically in cultivating an awareness of the indwelling Christ. We immerse ourselves in scripture not just to find solutions for problems or guidance in particular situations. We do it to saturate our minds with Jesus himself—who he was, what he did, how he acted—his spirit and style and attitudes. Put another way, we do this not just to pattern our lives after Jesus or to follow him; we do it to cultivate his indwelling presence. Following Jesus is important, but the experience of *being in Christ,* or having our lives hidden with Christ in God, is something else which gives us the power we need to follow Christ. The guiding presence of the indwelling Christ is implicit as we live our lives *in Christ,* and/or allow him to live in us.

That is the dynamic that makes possible other persons being sources of guidance. Alive in Christ, we can be Christ to and/or receive Christ from every person we meet.

Often I will begin a retreat by having persons share a love greeting. I ask them to select some one they don't know very well or not at all, get the person's first name, and exchange a greeting in this fashion. In pairs, they stand facing each other, holding both hands of each other, looking each other directly in the eye, and saying, "Mary, the love of Jesus in me greets the love of Jesus in you, and brings us together in the name of the Father, the Son, and the Holy Spirit." Then the other person shares the same greeting, I instruct them ahead of time to sit quietly after each has shared the greeting, without any comment, reflecting on what they are feeling. It is amazing how the mood changes. It is not unusual to see tears in people's eyes and have persons witness to a vivid awareness of the presence of Christ.

To be sure, this is in a special setting, but it at least suggests an ever-present possibility. John A. T. Robinson said, "The Christian cannot look into a human face without seeing Jesus and cannot look into Jesus' face without seeing God." The more we cultivate our awareness of the indwelling Christ, the more we resonate to his aliveness in others and discern his guidance through them. Also, the more sensitive we are to his presence, the more perceptive we are to the pain and need of others which present calls to our lives (*AC*, pp. 86–87).

Reflecting and Recording

Can you recall an experience during the past month when some other person helped you discern God's guidance? Make some notes here and on the next page about that experience. What was the issue? Why did you seek that particular person out, or did he/she come into your life "accidentally"? If you sought him/her out, why? What led you to that person?

✳ ✳ ✳

Spend a few minutes enjoying the fact that the indwelling Christ is a guiding presence. Offer your specific thanks for his guidance.

During the Day

To be guided by the indwelling Christ, we must stay aware of his presence. We must also be alert to and watch for the guidance that comes directly from him, from scripture, and from others. Then we must follow the guidance when it comes. Remember these principles as you move ahead in your life in Christ. Begin by making conscious use of these principles today.

Day Six: *A Creating Presence*

There may be little distinction between guiding and creating in the way the indwelling Christ shapes our lives. But we talk about them separately simply for focus.

One of the great discoveries of my life is that the indwelling Christ is a presence that stimulates, empowers, even directs the creative thrust of my spirit. When I dedicate the gifts God has given me to [God], when I am willing to turn loose, as it were, and allow the Spirit to flow, I am amazed at what happens. The indwelling Christ is a creating presence. I see myself as a rather disciplined person, at least in most areas. I am disciplined in my study, disciplined in work schedules, disciplined in my attention to family relations and responsibilities, somewhat disciplined in my devotional life. I am a diligent worker and believe work is an important part of the life process. I am certain, however, that the energizing vitality for what comes from my life these days is from the creating presence of the indwelling Christ (*AC*, pp. 89–90).

Paul was expressing this conviction, and witnessing to the creating, renewing power of Christ when he wrote the Corinthians: "We have this treasure in earthen vessels, to show that the transcendent power belongs to God and not to us" (2 Cor. 4:7, RSV).

My wife, Jerry, is an artist with much less formal training than most artists, but with a great reservoir of natural gifts. She is very deliberate about allowing the creating presence of the indwelling Christ to work within her. Her meditation/prayer experience is very explicit. She immerses herself in Scripture that affirms the love, concern, and power of Christ at work within her. She makes three specific petitions. One, that she will be open to Christ's creative inspiration and guidance. Two, that she will be led to the resources to equip her for the task—either her past learning, training and experience, or persons or resources who can be helpful in that particular task. Three, that she will love and trust herself and what comes from her designing, painting, and drawing, confident to express herself as well as possible, then in her words, "let it go."

The third movement in her preparation is a kind of meditation. Having immersed herself in affirmation from Scripture, and having prayed very specifically, she relaxes for twenty or thirty minutes, awake but in an almost-sleep, she empties herself in order to receive what Christ has to offer. From that relaxed receptivity, she proceeds with her work. She is confident that the indwelling Christ works creatively within her. Knowing her—her long, arduous battle with deep feelings of inadequacy and low self-esteem—I am convinced that this is the saving dynamic of her life—the creating presence of the indwelling Christ.

Do not mistake what I am saying. We are gifted in many different ways, each person uniquely so. We are endowed with talents and natural gifts. Apart from natural endowments the Holy Spirit also gives specific and different gifts to different people. Paul's word is applicable in either case: "The gifts we possess differ as they are allotted to us by God's grace, and must be exercised accordingly" (Rom. 12:6 NEB). The likelihood of my ever painting like Jerry, or

Jerry writing a workbook on prayer is rare—but the indwelling Christ works creatively in each of us (*AC,* pp. 92–93).

Reflecting and Recording

One of the ways the indwelling Christ works creatively within us is by giving us inner desire, by intensifying our drive to make new, to start over, to do his will. Paul put it in these words: "God is at work in you, both to will and to work for his good pleasure" (Phil. 2:13, RSV). The psalmist expressed the same thought. "Take delight in the Lord, and he will give you the desires of your heart" (Psalm 37:4, RSV).

Make a list of some of the primary desires of your life, what you want most, what you are trying to accomplish, some goals that you have. Put down four or five in a few words:

1.

2.

3

4.

Check the list now. Have you sought the creative power of the indwelling Christ in relation to them? Are they the kinds of desires and goals Christ would affirm? Which ones are you willing to commit to him for his perfecting and realizing?

✳ ✳ ✳

During the Day

Frederick Herzog stimulated in me the idea that the result of the creating presence of the indwelling Christ is not an *imitation of Christ* which can easily become superficial and counterfeit. It is a creating power which allows free expression and fulfillment of our unique selves. So it is not an *imitatio Christi,* imitation of Christ, but an *innovatio Christi,* and innovation of Christ, a fresh expression of Christ through each of us.

Move through this day not trying to *imitate* Christ, but being a fresh expression of his presence.

Day Seven: *The Creating Power of Struggle, Suffering, and Pain*

A book could be written, indeed books have been written, on both the guiding and creating power of Christ. This workbook is just a "taste," to some degree a hint, of what is possible. The emphasis this week has been a call to pursue the process of cultivating awareness of Christ as a guiding and creating presence. We close the week by focusing on struggle, suffering, and pain as the points at which Christ may do his most creative work.

A friend wrote me a power-packed letter about the supportive fellowship of her Christian friends and the direction she was finding in her personal prayer life and the fellowship of prayer in which she was participating.

> I would be less than truthful if I didn't say that it is a very difficult time for the Whitakers. We are still dealing with the trauma of Whit's loss of his job—the anger, the resentment, the "Why us?" rises in us from time to time like some kind of specter that will not die. It is just here that you helped me so tremendously. As I learn to use prayer not only as an access to my Father but as a *defense* against "the forces that would destroy his loving plan" for my life. When the negatives begin to surface, it is then that I am able to turn them over to him and overcome destructive forces in my life. I feel so often that I am in the midst of an unfolding drama, sometimes busy as a participant in it, very involved in my part, then again as an observer watching the whole thing with a sense of objectivity. *Very* strange, *very* exciting, very *scary.* I feel caught up in some kind of cosmic event much larger than I am but involving me personally and explicitly. All of this does not always make sense to me, but I am very aware that there is purpose and order to it and that God is using all of this to create in me something very worthwhile. It is what I prayed at the beginning and in that sense I am very much tuned in to the fact that God is not going to waste any of this. This is very philosophical and deeper than I normally try to share, but with you somehow it seems easy.
>
> On the practical side, we struggle with the financial part of it, the

tendency to self-pity, the desire to throw in the towel and give up. Decisions are hard to make and what is the worst is that sometimes we find that our anger is directed at *each other*. When that happens, and we catch it, thank God we can say ''I'm sorry'' and go on. Pray for us, Maxie. Particularly now Whit needs reassurance of his worth as a person, and we need patience to wait upon the Lord.

There is a lot there—so very much—but focus on two sentences. ''God is using all of this to create in me something very worthwhile. . . .God is not going to waste any of this.''

The mystery of suffering is insolvable. To even introduce the idea for a one day focus in this workbook may be unfair. Yet there is no evading the fact of suffering, and there is no solving of the mystery. So, I hope that suggesting one handle for living with it will be justifiable and will also make your grappling with it creative.

There are two primary responses we make: *rebellion* and *resignation*. Both have some merit. For instance, we are to rebel if rebellion means struggle. Especially is this true in our praying. One stance of prayer is *wrestling*. Paul says that when we don't know how we ought to pray, God's spirit ''intercedes for us with groans that words cannot express'' (Rom. 8: 26, NIV). He also wrote to the Ephesians, ''Our struggle is not against flesh and blood, but against the rulers, against the authorities, against the powers of this dark world and against the spiritual forces of evil in the heavenly realms (Eph. 6:12, NIV).

So we rebel and we wrestle. In prayer, especially, we struggle to understand, we join with God to fight against evil and sin and sickness and suffering. But rebellion as our only, or primary response to suffering, will lead to resentment and bitterness.

Resignation is another common response. If resignation is the passive giving in to whatever is, it will destroy our spirits. But if resignation is the active yielding of ourselves to Christ, the willingness for him to set the pace and lead the way, the positive joining of our strength with his in surrender to his will, then resignation becomes a creative force.

A movement between rebellion and resignation, the rhythm of which is set by acceptance, will make suffering, struggle, and pain creative. By *acceptance* I do not mean that God causes or initiates pain and suffering. God allows it and uses it for our good and God's glory. So we accept suffering as a part of life where God has given us freedom and called us to be responsible, in a world where unexplainable evil is obviously present. *Under these conditions,* we offer our suffering to Christ, and we believe with my friend that God will use it to ''create in me something new and worthwhile'' and that God will not waste any of our suffering and struggle.

Reflecting and Recording

Can you recall an experience of suffering and struggle in which Christ was a creating presence? You discovered strength and gifts you didn't know you had. You accomplished things that before you would not have believed possible. Write about that experience here.

If you are sharing this workbook venture with others, your meeting will probably be today. One creative way Christ uses our struggles and sufferings is in witness and relation to others. Perhaps you will be willing to share your experience with your group.

During the Day

Is there someone you know who is suffering a great deal or is in some sort of intense struggle? What can you do today to affirm that person? Decide now, and do it sometime today.

Is there someone, other than your workbook group, maybe the one you've just thought about, who would perhaps profit from you sharing the experience of struggle you wrote of above? Do you need to see that person or call on the phone or write a letter? (Remember what we talked about two days ago—we are guided by others).

Group Meeting for Week Five

Introduction

The theme of this week has been the guiding and creating presence of the indwelling Christ. It was noted clearly that we are guided by others; that others may be the source of discerning God's will for our lives. Also interchange with others, dynamic relationships, stimulate creativity.

That is why these sharing sessions are very important. Don't underestimate the value of each person's contribution.

Sharing Together

1. Begin your time together by the leader offering an opening prayer or calling on someone else (consulted ahead of time) to do so. Then sing a chorus or a couple of verses of a hymn everyone knows.

2. Ask each person to share the most meaningful insight or experience gained from this week.

3. On Day Two, I shared an experience of guidance. Invite as many persons who will to take two or three minutes to share some experience. Suggest that everyone review what he/she wrote in response to such a question in the reflecting and recording time on Day Two. As each person shares, note the way guidance came. Was it directly from Christ, from scripture, from other ideas in their mind, God placing something in their imagination?

4. On Day Four, our focus was prayer as a source of guidance, and some of the problems we have with prayer. Two common experiences are that we feel something is wrong with us when God doesn't seem to be responding to our praying, or we suspect people claim far more about the effectiveness of prayer than they actually experience. Spend ten or fifteen minutes discussing these as you have experienced them, and what responses we may make to persons who tell us that is their experience.

5. Guidance comes through persons. Invite persons to share specifically how they have discerned God's guidance through some other person. Hopefully at least two or three persons will share.

6. The indwelling Christ as a creating presence is not a notion we talk a lot about. Acknowledge this, discuss it a bit, then ask if any person can share such an experience.

7. Focus now on struggle, suffering, and pain. Ask persons to share an experience of struggle or pain out of which something positive, creative, and good came.

Praying Together

Spontaneous conversational prayer is a creative and guiding source in our corporate life. Close your time together by inviting as many as will to offer brief prayers growing out of your sharing tonight. Before you begin this, ask if anyone in the group has specific prayer requests, especially areas where guidance is being sought.

When as many as wish to have prayed, close by inviting all to pray together the Lord's Prayer.

A Converting Presence

Day One: *A Converting Presence*

> May the God of peace make you holy through and through. May you be kept in soul and mind and body in spotless integrity until the coming of our Lord Jesus Christ. He who calls you is utterly faithful and he will finish what he has set out to do.
>
> —1 Thessalonians 5:23–24, PHILLIPS

This prayer of Paul's offers a sparkling possibility—to be holy (whole) through and through. This is the work of the indwelling Christ, shaping us in wholeness. *Integrity* means integrated, to be "in one piece." Paul includes all that we are in this shaping work of the "God of peace"—soul and mind and body.

The process is a continuing one, but it will be finished. "He who calls you is utterly faithful and he will finish what he set out to do." So we concentrate for a few days on the indwelling Christ as a *converting* presence.

It is a commentary on our failure to be clear in communicating the gospel that I struggled for the right word here. *Converting* is a rather specialized word, in religion and other disciplines. It is a common word in physics, chemistry, and engineering—conversion of energy, of materials, of solids to liquids, liquids to solids, gases to fire and heat and cold. Though a common word in religious language, it is not common in usage today, and to a marked degree has lost its power. We have allowed narrow fundamentalists to restrict and distort its meaning. Not being willing to be squeezed into that mold, we have given up one of our most powerful and descriptive words.

We have even gone further in many quarters of the church. Not only have we given up the word, we have diminished a cardinal principle of the gospel which the word describes. We simply do not think much within the church about conversion. When we think about it, too often we use it to designate only that beginning point of our salvation when we accept God's gracious love in Jesus Christ and are justified through our faith in God's sacrificial gift for our sins (*AC,* p. 97).

Two things happened in *the fall* and in our *own fall.* One, we became estranged from God; two, God's image within us was broken, distorted, defaced. See how this harmonizes with our focus of Day Three of Week Four: "Good news, bad news, good news"—the good news of creation in the image of God, the bad news of sin and the loss of God-created image, and the good news of re-creation. "If anyone is in Christ, he is a new creation" (2 Cor. 5:17, RSV). The indwelling Christ is a converting presence, finishing what God set forth to do.

Reflecting and Recording

The term "born again Christian" is a popular one in our day. Why do you, or why do you think others, feel a need to refer to themselves as "born again Christians"?

✳   ✳   ✳

Of the persons you know who would refer to themselves as born again Christians, what would be primary characteristics of their lives? Make some notes.

In the context of the gospel, to use the term "born again" to describe a Christian is redundant. To be born again is to be a Christian; to be a Christian is to be born again. The indwelling Christ is a converting presence, restoring and renewing that distorted and defaced image within us. We can speak of being born again because it is that dramatic.

Look at your own experience. You may want to go back to Days One and Two of Week One when you were asked to reflect on receiving the justifying grace of God. Do you see that experience, or any other experience of your life, as being a born-again-experience? Record your feelings and observations here.

Is there a sense in which you can say that being born again is an ongoing experience? Ponder the thought and then thank the living Christ for all his transforming work in your life.

✳   ✳   ✳

During the Day

Deliberately engage two or three persons today in talking about their Christian experience. You'll have to model and stimulate by talking about your own experience. Pay attention to the images and symbols they use in referring to new life and change.

Day Two: *Being Born Again—and Again*

There is in the Christian experience of salvation a discontinuity between what was and what now is.
Spend a minute or two reflecting on this thought.

✳   ✳   ✳

Yesterday, I contended that to be Christian is to be born again, and to be born again is to be Christian. You remember the dramatic encounter of Jesus with Nicodemus.

Now there was a man of the Pharisees, named Nicodemus, a ruler of the Jews. This man came to Jesus by night and said to him, "Rabbi, we know that you are a teacher come from God; for no one can do these signs that you do, unless God is with him." Jesus answered him, "Truly, truly, I say to you, unless one is born anew, he cannot see the kingdom of God." Nicodemus said to him, 'How can a man be born when he is old? Can he enter a second time into his mother's womb and be born?" Jesus answered, "Truly, truly, I say to you, unless one is born of water and the Spirit, he cannot enter the kingdom of God. That which is born of the flesh is flesh, and that which is born of the Spirit is spirit. Do not marvel that I said to you, 'You must be born anew' "

—John 3:1–7, RSV.

To be born again, Jesus said to Nicodemus, is a *must*, not an option. The experience is not our own doing; it is the Spirit working in us. We are not saved by our own moral self-improvement, or by refining our belief system, or by doing and being better and better. We are saved by allowing Christ's power to work radically within us.

Thus the first statement of today: *There is in the Christian experience of salvation a discontinuity between what was and what now is.* We begin at this point in our understanding of the gospel, for unless we begin here, there is no place to go. But let this be equally clear: if the Christian experience ends here, it ends. We are to be born again—yes, and again and again. The indwelling Christ is a converting presence.

Here is a parable of the truth from the remarkable musician, Pablo Casals.

> Each day I am reborn. Each day I must begin again. For the past 80 years I have started each day in the same manner. It is not a mechanical routine but something essential to my life. I go to the piano and I play two preludes and fugues of Bach. I cannot think of doing otherwise. It is a benediction on the house. But that is not its only meaning for me. It is a rediscovery of the world of which I have the joy of being a part. It fills me with the wonder of eternity, with the incredible miracle of God. The music is never the same for me. Each day is something new, fantastic, unbelievable!

So it is as we yielded ourselves to the converting presence of the indwelling Christ. The "Music" is never the same, since we have "put off the old nature with its practices and have put on the new nature, *which is being renewed . . .* after the image of its creator" (Col. 3:10, italics mine). It takes time—a lifetime, really—to come to spiritual maturity, to grow up "to the measure of the stature of the fulness of Christ" (Eph. 4:13). But how exciting—to know that it can happen, and to feel the power of it and see the effects of its happening in my own life. The indwelling Christ is a converting presence (*AC*, p. 108).

Reflecting and Recording

In Week One on Day Two, you were asked to do a timeline plotting some special times when God was working in your life. These times probably centered around specific and significant experiences. Go back and look at what you wrote, and reflect on these two thoughts as they relate to your experience.

1. There is in the Christian experience of salvation a discontinuity between what was and what is now.

2. We are to be born again—yes, and again and again.

✳   ✳   ✳

During the Day

You were asked yesterday to engage two or three persons in talking about their Christian experience. Did you? If you did or didn't, do so today. As you pay attention to the images and symbols they use, see how they fit into the two thoughts you were just asked to reflect upon.

On page 173, there is a tent-card with this affirmation: There is in the Christian experience of salvation a discontinuity between what was and what now is. Cut it out, fold it, and put it in a place where not only you will see it, but where others may see it and raise questions. Be prepared to talk about the meaning of this statement.

Day Three: *Affirming Presence*

That we bear God's image, that we are created in the likeness of God, is the claim of scripture over and over again. "Then God said, 'Let us make man in our image' " (Gen. 1:26, RSV). "What is man that thou art mindful of him. . . . Yet thou hast made him little less than God" (Psalm 8:4–5, RSV). "Be perfect, therefore, as your heavenly Father is perfect" (Matt. 5:48, NIV). "The glory which thou [God] hast given me I have given to them. . . . I in them and thou in me" (John 17:22–23, RSV). "Here and now, dear friends, we are God's children; what we shall be has not yet been disclosed, but we know that when it is disclosed we shall be like him, because we shall see him as he is" (1 John 3:2, NEB).

It is crucially important in spiritual formation to connect the working of the indwelling Christ as a *converting* presence with his work as an *affirming* presence. They go together. The indwelling Christ affirms our beings as persons. The human creature is good. Someone put it in the vernacular: "God made me, and God don't make no trash!" One of the church fathers, Irenaeus, cast it in an unforgettable sentence: "The glory of God is man fully alive."

Unfortunately much of the classic teaching in the area of spiritual formation has focused narrowly on disciplines that were to mortify, suppress, even "kill," some of our basic human drives or attributes. Thus most Christian spirituality prior to the twentieth century has been primarily ascetic. It divided our nature, staging battles between "flesh" and spirit, seeking to cultivate the spirit at the expense of the body. Thus our primary model of spirituality has been the *ascetic* one. Throughout the history of the Roman Catholic Church, the monastic calling has been seen as the highest vocation. Though not as tenaciously held, the idea persists today.

And it is not restricted to the Roman Church. All Christian spirituality has been shaped by the great spiritual classics such as *The Imitation of Christ*. With telling consistency, these classics sought to teach us how to suppress our normal drives and desires and so strengthen the spirit. The Puritan expression of Christianity which has infused all of Protestantism was almost as world denying as monasticism (*AC*, p.100).

This ascetic approach to spiritual formation is rooted in the confusion of Paul's New Testament language about body and soul or flesh and spirit which we considered on Day Four of Week Three. Some inconsistencies in translating the New Testament as a result of Greek influence led to a dualism of flesh and spirit in early Christian thought. What emerged was the perception of an ongoing struggle between the divine Spirit and our bodies, and between our "lower" and "higher" natures. It was the lingering effect of Greek thought that led to the unfortunate translation of Romans 8 where "flesh' becomes "lower nature" in the New English Bible. The whole of Paul's writings lead me to believe this is precisely what he did not mean.

Though we addressed this issue briefly before, it is so crucial that we must look at it again to get the perspective clear.

Paul was a Hebrew, rooted in Hebrew thought in which a division of *man* into lower and higher natures was almost wholly absent. In Hebrew thought, *flesh* was not an element of the self at war with some "higher" element; it was the whole of human existence. So you have Isaiah's promise that "the glory of the Lord shall be revealed, and *all flesh* shall see it together" (40:5, italics mine). Following that he says, "All flesh is grass" and withers (v.6), "but the word of our God will stand for ever'' (v. 8). Human life is transient, Isaiah is saying. So I repeat an earlier word: Flesh is not a neutral term describing a "nature" or our "essence." It is an evaluative term describing the transitory, temporary dimensions of our existence, the fact of the weakness, finiteness, and vulnerability of our earthly sojourn. Flesh and sin are not to be equated. Paul contrasts flesh and spirit in describing the way we live. Spirit and flesh are domains of power, spheres of influence in which one lives. Sin is closely linked to flesh because flesh is the domain of power where sin operates. Paul condemns sin, not flesh. God came in Christ to enter the domain of flesh in order that sin might be conquered once and for all.

This understanding and conviction gives clarity to Paul's continuous contention that there was no salvation by *law*. Law operates in the domain of flesh, where we live without the transforming power of the indwelling Christ. In the flesh, we are impotent to keep the law. How vividly real to our own experience is Paul's testimony in Romans 8:1–6 when we read it in this light.

There is therefore now no condemnation for those who are in Christ Jesus. For the law of the Spirit of life in Christ Jesus has set me free from the law of sin and death. For God has done what the law, weakened by the flesh, could not do: sending his own Son in the likeness of sinful flesh and for sin, he condemned sin in the flesh, in order that the just requirement of the law might be fulfilled in us, who walk not according to the flesh but according to the Spirit. For those who live according to the flesh set their minds on the things of the flesh, but those who live according to the Spirit set their minds on the things of the Spirit. To set the mind on the flesh is death, but to set the mind on the Spirit is life and peace. (Rom. 8:1-6)

This is the key that unlocks the door to vital Christian living—the powerful dynamic of *the Spirit of life in Christ Jesus that frees us.* For those who live according to the flesh set their minds on the things of the flesh, but those who live according to the Spirit, set their minds on the things of the Spirit. The perspective is important. Our predicament is not that we are *in the flesh,* but that we want to live *according* to the flesh, that is setting our minds on "the flesh" as a domain of power. Jesus is not at war with our humanity. The destruction of our human nature is not the goal of Christ-living, but conversion—the conversion of our feelings, drives, passions, instincts.

There is no question. When we are honest, most of us readily confess with Paul that there is "a war going on in my members." We *will* to do something, but find ourselves doing just the opposite. For some of us, the inner conflict is a full-scale war. For others, who have been on the way for some time, it may be more like guerrilla warfare, with pockets of enemy forces holding out here and there, moving in for episodic confrontations. This is why we must experience the indwelling Christ as a converting presence and power. Also, we must realize that we need a series of conversions. The new life that has come to birth within us is a process of conversion, through which the power of the indwelling Christ brings all the powers of our being, all the feelings, instincts, drives, and passions into wholeness. These powers are not suppressed or pummeled into subjection; they are focused, coordinated, harnessed—in a word, converted to constructive expressions of our new life in Christ (*AC*, pp. 102–3).

Reflecting and Recording

We have dealt with more content today than usual. So would you simply sit quietly for a moment and allow Paul's word to pervade your *thinking* and feeling. "For the law of the Spirit of life in Christ Jesus has set me free from the law of sin and death" (Rom. 8:2, RSV).

※   ※   ※

During the Day

As you move through the day, pay attention to how you handle your feelings, drives, instincts. Do you deny, suppress, put down? Do you see them as *good* or *bad*?

Day Four: *Every Weed a Potential Flower*

To deal with the feelings, drives, instincts, and passions of our life which need to be converted would require at least an entire book. Our love needs converting because love can be perverted. Our sexual drives need converting because sex is too often kept at a base level of animal heat, rather than transformed into an expression of love and self-giving. Our acquisitive instincts need converting because too often this instinct turns into selfish grasping of any and everything we desire. Our instinct for survival needs converting. This is one of our most basic needs and it drives us to hoard our resources, to lock, ourselves within ourselves, never becoming vulnerable, never risking self-disclosure, ordering our entire lives after the model of a limited bank account against which we are afraid to draw lest we give out too soon. Pride, without which we often become sluggards or are overcome with self-depreciation, even self-hatred, and with which we often become self-centered egotists, needs converting. What J. Wallace Hamilton labels the ''drum-major instinct,'' needs converting. This is a drive that encompasses many different expressions, most of which are in the forefront of our lives at one time or another. It is a retinue of drives and feelings attendant to the passion *to be first* in line.

I could go on, and so could you, up or down the scale according to who is making the list: the need to belong, the fear of failure, the craving for attention, the passion for security, the obsession for power, the pull of adventure, the lure of mystery, the yearning for community, the longing for intimacy, the lust for sexual satisfaction, the seductive power of glamour, the craving for comfort, the pull of the familiar.

What do we do with ourselves? How do we deal with these hordes of feelings and passions? We recognize them and name them if we can. We affirm that they are a part of who we are. They are not evil shoots to be uprooted and cast away, or wild tares foreign to the harvest of a healthy personality. J. Wallace Hamilton in *Ride the Wild Horses!* puts it well:

Jesus is not at war with our human nature. He does not say that our instincts were born of evil or that our only hope is to cast them out, or to beat them down. He understood perfectly, in the realm of plant nature: that every weed is a potential flower, and that the very qualities which make it a weed could make it a flower. Great sinners and great saints contain much the same stuff.

The indwelling Christ is a converting presence. This converting aspect of his shaping power is connected with his affirming work. His converting and affirming presence work together to bring wholeness. Every aspect of our being is to be yielded to the converting power of the indwelling Christ. Obviously we are talking about a process that requires time. Recall our working understanding of spiritual formation: the dynamic process of receiving by faith and appropriating through commitment, discipline, and action, the living Christ into our life to the end that our life will conform to, and manifest the reality of Christ's presence in the world. The claim is bold and extravagant—that we can so live with Christ, so cultivate the awareness of his presence within us, and so yield ourselves to his shaping power that we can become persons who reflect his likeness (*AC,* pp. 103–5).

Reflecting and Recording

The following are some feelings, drives, instincts, or passions common to us: love, acquisitiveness, instinct for survival, pride. Select a couple of these and list them on the lines below. In the space provided, write some reflections on how these need to be transformed and/or directed by the converting presence of the indwelling Christ. You need to be honest about how these feelings, drive, or instincts are presently being expressed.

1.

2.

During the Day

Put into practice what you have concluded in your above reflections. Be careful that you don't make this a do-it-yourself project. You must willfully decide and act, but remember we are talking about the shaping power of the indwelling Christ. Call upon that presence, and/or yield to it as necessary.

Day Five: *Rhythm of the Christian Life*

For a During-the-Day suggestion yesterday, I asked you to remember that the changing and channeling of our feelings, drives, passions, and instincts are not a do-it-yourself project. The indwelling Christ is a converting presence, shaping our lives. I have contended all along that dying and rising with Christ is the rhythm of the Christian life.

Prayer and spiritual formation is the deliberate, intentional effort to live our whole life in the context of the life, death, and resurrection of Jesus. Our *union* with Christ is in death and resurrection. Pascal said, ''It is one of the greatest principles of Christianity that that which happened in Jesus Christ may happen in the soul of the Christian. We have a linking not only with Calvary, but with his resurrection.'' Commitment to Christ is to die to flesh as the domain of power controlling our lives; that is to die to *our own* control of our lives. Then we share Christ's resurrection, Christ lives in us and we experience being raised to a new level of living *under his guidance and by his power.*

There is a sense in which we are no longer in control, no longer in charge of our destiny. Sure, we continue to make decisions and we are always responsible. Yet, the process of conversion is the process of yielding every aspect of our lives, every drive, feeling, passion, and instinct, to the indwelling Christ every day.

There is an interesting phrase in this word of Paul to the Colossians (3:1–4), simple, easy to pass over, but packed with meaning: ''Christ who is our life.'' This is no incidental word for Paul. ''It is no longer I who live,'' he said, ''but Christ who lives in me'' (Gal. 2:20). ''For to me to live is Christ'' (Phil. 1:21). This claim of Paul to life in Christ is always connected with death and resurrection. ''If we have been united with him in a death like his, we shall certainly be united with him in a resurrection like his. . . . consider yourselves dead to sin and alive to God in Christ Jesus'' (Rom. 6:5, 11). Conversion then, the work of Christ within us, is the process of death and resurrection, with our ultimate hope being a final resurrection ''when Christ . . . appears, and we shall also . . . appear with him in glory'' (Col. 3:4) (*AC,* pp. 105–6).

Reflecting and Recording

Can you locate an experience in which you felt yourself being raised to a new level of power under the guidance and power of the indwelling Christ? Don't think only of the dramatic. Describe the experience.

During the Day

Continue to work on the two feelings or drives you reflected upon on Day Four. The process is primarily that of yielding these to the indwelling Christ every day.

Day Six: *Live Life as Jesus Lived It*

In 1966 a retrospective of Picasso's paintings was exhibited in Cannes, France. Hundreds of his works, from the first he did as an adolescent beginner to the latest of the master, who was then eight-five years old, graced the walls of the gallery. The old man himself roamed about, enjoying the show more than anyone. One report told of a woman who stopped him and said, "I don't understand. Over there, the beginning pictures—so mature, serious and solemn—then the later ones, so different, so irrepressible. It almost seems as though the dates should be reversed. How do you explain it?"

"Easily," replied Picasso, eyes sparkling. "It takes a long time to become young."

So it does!

To be alive in Christ is constant and continuous. We are not finished, but are "under construction," maturing into the "measure of the stature of the fullness of Christ." Conversion is an ongoing process which we must keep alive. What e.e. cummings said was true for everyone has particular meaning for Christians: "We can never be born enough. We are human beings for whom birth is a supremely welcome mystery, the mystery of becoming." This is the purpose of spiritual disciplines—to keep alive the conversion process, to fertilize the seeds of potential within so that new birth and growth will happen (*AC*, pp. 109–10).

It is essential that we talk about *keeping the conversion process alive*. *Maturing* is a more accurate description of a Christian than *mature*. There may be a few mature Christians around, but most of us are maturing Christians.

This is true, first, because in the whole of life, and especially in Christianity, there is no school where we learn the right answers and graduate to maturity. We never lose our capacity to learn. Second, maturity is not a matter of chronological age; it has to do with psychological, emotional, and spiritual growth. Three, if we think we have arrived, we've stopped growing; and to be growing is a mark of maturity.

Paul has a beautiful expression of this in his prayer for the Ephesians.

> I pray that the God of our Lord Jesus Christ, the all-glorious Father, may give you the spiritual powers of wisdom and vision, by which there comes the knowledge of him. I pray that your inward eyes may be illumined, so that you may know what is the hope to which he calls you, what the wealth and glory of the share he offers you among his people in their heritage, and how vast the resources of his power open to us who trust in him. They are measured by his strength and might which he exerted in Christ when he raised him from the dead.
> —Ephesians 1:17-20, NEB

The "share he offers" is our share in the life of Christ which is the heritage of all Christians. Paul talks about this in terms of our sharing in the resurrection of Christ. Henri Nouwen offers a challenging comment on Paul's prayer.

> This prayer makes clear that the spiritual life is a life guided by the same Spirit who guided Jesus Christ. The Spirit is the breath of Christ in us, the divine power of Christ active in us, the mysterious source of new vitality by which we are made aware that it is not we who live, but Christ who lives in us . . . Indeed, to live a spiritual life means to become living Christs. It is not enough to try to imitate Christ as much as possible; it is not enough to remind others of Jesus; it is not even enough to be inspired by the words and actions of Jesus Christ. No, the spiritual life presents us with a far more radical demand: to be living Christs here and now, in time and history (Nouwen, p. 13).

Radical? Yes. And more radical when we realize that this is the call not to particular persons, but to all who would be Christian. This is what it means to keep the conversion process alive. *The Christian life is life as Jesus lived it and now lives it in us.*

Reflecting and Recording

Get the focus clear. Throughout this week we have thought about the indwelling Christ as a converting presence. Today we have underscored the fact that conversion is a process that must be ongoing, and which we must keep alive.

We joined with that the goal toward which we are moving which will be our whole focus next week. Memorize this sentence. *The Christian life is life as Jesus lived it and now lives it in us.*

✳ ✳ ✳

Look back at the prayer Paul prayed for the Ephesians. Write that prayer in your own words with yourself as the focus. Pray for yourself what Paul prayed for the Ephesians.

During the Day

Take with you into this day the sentence above which you memorized. Keep that sentence always at the edge of your conscious awareness, and live accordingly. Register occasions when it is *natural,* as well as when you had to put forth deliberate effort to *live life as Jesus lived it.*

Day Seven: *Keeping the Conversion Process Alive*

Return to my definition of spiritual formation. Spiritual formation is that dynamic process of receiving through faith and appropriating through commitment, discipline, and action, the living Christ into our own life to the end that our life will conform to, and manifest the reality of Christ's presence in the world.

We keep the conversion process alive through *commitment, discipline,* and *action.*

Commitment is a daily need and act. Every day we renew our commitment to Christ, and we keep committing ourselves by saying yes to Christ. We will concentrate on action next week. We close this week with a brief look at discipline.

In 1984, The Upper Room published my book, *The Workbook on Spiritual Disciplines,* in which I dealt with some essential disciplines of the Christian life: study, scripture and guidance, prayer, confession, submission and service, solitude, and generosity. There are other important disciplines that involve worship and Christian community as well as the discipline of spiritual friendship which John Wesley called "Christian conferencing." There is also what Mr. Wesley called *prudential* means of grace or "works of mercy" on which we will focus on Day Three of next week.

We can't deal with these disciplines in this workbook; we can only underscore the necessity for them. We keep the conversion process alive by discipline. As we focus these disciplines on cultivating an awareness of the indwelling Christ, we are led to a form of spirituality that deserves a lot of attention . . . a spirituality that gives expression to the indwelling Christ. Remember, that's the end toward which we are moving in my definition of spiritual formation: that our life will conform to and manifest the reality of Christ's presence in the world.

I remember vividly a conversation I had with Anthony Bloom, the Russian Orthodox who has written so helpfully in the area of prayer (*Living Prayer, School of Prayer,* and *Courage to Pray,* all published by Darton, Longman & Todd, London). We were filming the conversation to use as a resource for teaching, especially in prayer groups, schools of prayer, and retreats. At one point we were talking about the connection between contemplation and action, and I asked Metropolitan Bloom to define contemplation. He responded.

Well I think this is where contemplation begins. Sit and listen—in religious terms it may be called waiting on God—but it's simply plain listening or looking in order to hear and to understand. If we did that with regard to the situations in which we are, to everything people say to us or what they are in life, with regard to our own selves—we would be in that condition which one can call contemplation, which consists in pondering, thinking deeply, in waiting until one has understood in order to act. Then action would be much more efficient, less hasty, and filled, probably, with some amount of the Divine Wisdom.

That is a clear definition, but he made it even clearer by using two images. One was a nursery rhyme he learned in the United States.

A Wise old owl
lived in an oak;
The more he saw
the less he spoke;
The less he spoke,
the more he heard.
Why can't we all be
like that bird?

His second image he borrowed from the English mystic and writer Evelyn Underhill. A Christian should be like a sheep dog. When the shepherd wants the dog to do something, the dog lies down at his master's feet, looks intently into the shepherd's eyes, and listens without budging until he has understood the mind of the master. Then he jumps to his feet and runs to do it. And, equally important, at no moment does the dog stop wagging its tail.

It is that sort of understanding that enables Bloom to write so simply and clearly, to apply the most profound truths about prayer and spirituality to our practical everyday situation. In his book *Courage to Pray* he illumines intercession and the connection between contemplation and action by talking about the role of Mary in Jesus' first miracle—the turning of water to wine in Cana (John 2:1–11). The story is confusing in many ways, especially in the disjointed conversation between Jesus and Mary. Mary told him that the hosts had run out of wine. In what mood Jesus responds we do not know, but his words are baffling, maybe even a rebuke: "Is that your concern or mine? What have you to do with me? My hour has not yet come." What grace Mary shows! She doesn't challenge Jesus, or question his kindness and compassion to her. She simply tells the servants to do whatever Jesus tells them.

Bloom says that instead of answering Jesus, Mary "brings the kingdom by showing she has perfect faith in him, that the words she has pondered in her heart from the beginning have been fruitful and she sees him for what he is, the word of God." Then Bloom makes an adroit and concrete application.

We too can be in the same situation as Mary. We too can make God's kingdom come, wherever we are, in spite of the unbelief of the people we are with. Simply by having complete faith in the Lord and thus showing ourselves to be children of the kingdom. This is a crucially important act of intercession. The fact that we are present in a situation alters it profoundly because God is then present with us through our faith. Wherever we are, at home with our family, with friends when a quarrel is about to begin, at work or even simply in the underground, the street, the train, we can recollect ourselves and say, 'Lord I believe in you, come and be among us.' And by this act of faith, in a contemplative prayer which does not ask to see, we can intercede with God who has promised his presence when we ask for it. Sometimes we have no words, sometimes we do not know how to act wisely, but we can always ask God to come and be present. And we shall see how often the atmosphere changes, quarrels stop, peace comes. This is not a minor mode of intercession, although it is less spectacular than a great sacrifice. We see in it again how contemplation and action are inseparable, that Christian action is impossible without contemplation. We see also how such contemplation is not a vision of God alone, but a deep vision of everything enabling us to see its eternal meaning. Contemplation is a vision not of God alone, but of the world in God. (*Courage to Pray*)

We keep the process of conversion alive by this sort of contemplative living (*AC*, pp. 123–25).

Reflecting and Recording

Since you have had a heavy load of content today, simply sit quietly, and reflect on what you have read. You may want to go back and reread some of it.

✳   ✳   ✳

Commitment is daily business. Commit yourself anew to Christ now.

✳   ✳   ✳

During the Day

The ongoing process of Christian commitment is saying yes to Christ in every way possible every day. Note the times today that you have to *struggle* to say yes. But decide now you will do it, however difficult.

Group Meeting for Week Six

Introduction

You are drawing to the close of this workbook venture. This and your next meeting will be the last planned group meetings. Your group may want to discuss the future. Would the group like to stay together for a longer time? Are there resources (books, tapes, etc.) that the group would like to use corporately? If you are a part of the same church, is there some way you might share the experience you have had with others? Test the group to see if they would like to discuss future possibilities.

Sharing Together.

1. Leader, begin the session by praying aloud Paul's prayer from First Thessalonians 5, with which you began Week Six.

2. Ask persons to respond to this statement: As Christians, there is a sense in which we are no longer in charge of our destiny. The process of conversion is the process of yielding every aspect of our lives, every drive, feeling, passion, and instinct to the indwelling Christ. Encourage all to respond, to express questions and reservations, and especially to talk about any unwillingness or resistance to the process of conversion.

3. Spend ten to fifteen minutes talking about being born again. To be sensitive to each other, do not become argumentative. You can escape this trap by focusing on personal experience. Center on persons sharing what they may consider their born-again experience and talking about the sense in which being born again is an ongoing experience. You may begin the discussion by persons responding to the statement that to describe someone as a "born again Christian" is redundant.

4. In your reflecting and recording for Day Five, you were asked to locate a personal experience in which you felt yourself being raised to a new level of power under the guidance of the indwelling Christ. Invite three or four persons to share such an experience. Ask the group to note the variety of experiences, as well as the different channels of guidance and power.

5. If time allows, invite persons in the group to share any concern raised by this week's involvement. Since there is only one other group gathering, if time allows, ask for concerns and questions arising out of the past six weeks.

Praying Together

1. Ask someone to volunteer sharing with the group the prayer he/she wrote on Day Six in response to Paul's prayer for the Ephesians.

2. On Day Four of this past week, persons were asked to name two feelings, drives, instincts or passions in their own life in need of the converting and directing power of the indwelling Christ. Close your prayer period in a time of silent prayer. Invite persons to share aloud a need in their life in this area. After a person shares, spend a time of silent prayer for that person before another shares. This should be spontaneous as the group sits quietly with eyes closed.

When all who wish have shared, the leader may verbalize a brief prayer to close the meeting.

Being Christ

Day One: *One in Whom Christ Is Felt to Live Again*

I have said it a number of different ways: *being spiritually formed as Christians means being conformed to Christ's life, so that our lives manifest the reality of his presence in the world.* Stop for a moment now and reflect on this truth—especially that our lives might manifest the reality of his presence in the world.

✳ ✳ ✳

During this final week of our alive-in-Christ journey, we are concentrating on *being Christ to others*. Prayer and prayerful living is recognizing and cultivating the awareness of Christ's presence and expressing that presence in the world.

Malcolm Muggeridge closed his biography of Mother Teresa of Calcutta with this word:

It will be for posterity to decide whether she is a saint. I only say of her that in a dark time she is a burning and a shining light; in a cruel time, a living embodiment of Christ's gospel of love; in a godless time, the Word dwelling among us, full of grace and truth. *(Something Beautiful for God)*

I assume Muggeridge is using the word *saint* in a specialized way. For me I see no need to leave the question for posterity. The Christian saint is a Christian individual in full degree. That is the end toward which we all move—*to be Christian in full degree,* and

153

that means to be alive in Christ. Jacopone da Todi put it clearly: a saint is "one in whom Christ is felt to live again." Mother Teresa would not claim it, but her life is a transparent witness of it, and her words have the ring of authenticity because of who she is and what she does. Hear her.

Because we cannot see Christ we cannot express our love to him; but our neighbours we can always see, and we can do to them what if we saw him we would like to do to Christ. . . .

It is a danger, if we forget to whom we are doing it. Our works are only an expression of our love for Christ. Our hearts need to be full of love for him and since we have to express that love in action, naturally then the poorest of the poor are the means of expressing our love for God. . . .

Because it is a continual contact with Christ in his work, it is the same contact we have during Mass and in the Blessed Sacrament. There we have Jesus in the appearance of bread. But here in the slums, in the broken body, in the children, we see Christ and we touch him. (*Something Beautiful for God*) (*AC,* pp. 133–34).

As Christians we are to be those "in whom Christ is felt to live again." What Christ has been and done for us we must be and do for others.

Reflecting and Recording

Can you name three persons in whom Christ is felt to live again? Write their names in the blanks.

1._____

2._____

3._____

In the space below these names, write a few sentences about these persons describing why you see Christ in them. Do that now.

* * *

From what you have written, pick our five or six words which describe these persons.

_____ , _____ , _____

_____ , _____ , _____

Offer a prayer of gratitude for these persons.

During the Day

If any of the persons you listed above are living, call them by phone, or write them a letter, telling them about this experience of reflection and how you feel that Christ lives in them.

Day Two: *Something Beautiful for God*

Malcolm Muggeridge titled his biography of Mother Teresa from which we quoted yesterday *Something Beautiful for God*. That's what Christians are to be. One of Mother Teresa's words from the quote yesterday was that ''our works are only an expression of our love for Christ.''

Sometimes we see that clearly. I have a dear friend in whom I have seen it recently.

Abel Hendricks has been the President of the Methodist Church in South Africa twice and was the recipient of the 1980 World Methodist Peace Prize. He and his wife Freda received the 1986 Upper Room Citation. They are among the most dedicated Christians I know.

Abel has been in jail a number of times for his opposition to apartheid and for his commitment to solidarity with the poor and the

Blacks of South Africa. He is identified by that government as "Colored" which, in the rigid and oppressive social structure of South Africa, is one step above the status of Blacks in a nation whose political system denies almost every basic human right to the vast majority of her population.

As an effort to offer a morsel of appeasement, the South African government established two houses of parliament other than the all-white house that still controls. One is for Coloreds and one for Asians— neither of which will have any ultimate power. Abel could have probably won a seat in the parliament of this new system. But his understanding of and commitment to the tremendous majority who continue to be oppressed led him to oppose the proposed system.

The Hendricks are poor; they have no security. In the midst of the struggle about the parliament, white leaders come to Abel urging him to rescind a pastoral letter he'd written to the people of his district in which he invited them to boycott the election of these new houses of parliament as an expression of love and solidarity with the poor and as a witness against apartheid.

The white government leaders thought they could get to Abel by appealing to his self-interests. He is not many years away from retirement, has no property of his own, a very uncertain future. They offered him a retirement home, fully paid for, if he would simply "be quiet."

I'm sure it was with one of the most disarming smiles the officials had ever seen, illuminating a humility that resonates a sense of confidence and power, because that's who Abel is. He withstood the temptation.

"In my Father's house are many mansions," he said. "I dare not risk losing my house in heaven for anything you might offer me on earth."

Where is the source of such power, such clarity of conviction and commitment to a people for whom Abel has chosen to do battle? The indwelling Christ is shaping Abel's life. He is living life as Jesus lived it and now lives it in him.

In a telephone conversation, I was seeking to encourage and strengthen Abel on an occasion when he had just been released from jail. Instead, he encouraged and strengthened me. He quoted Paul, and never have the words had such powerful meaning. "It is not I who lives, Christ lives in me. . . . I can do all things through his strength."

Reflecting and Recording

Yesterday you were asked to pick five or six words which described the persons in whom you felt Christ was alive again. Review and list those words at the top of the next page.

——————————, ——————————, ——————————

——————————, ——————————, ——————————

Be honest now. This is between you and the Lord. Don't be falsely humble. Which of these words characterize your life, at least in part. (Remember we are not mature but maturing.) Put a check mark by those words.

* * *

Which of the persons you listed yesterday as "one in whom Christ is felt to live again" are you most attracted to? Why? Think about it for a while.

* * *

Of the five or six one-word characteristics listed above, which ones do you most need to cultivate? List them here.

Prayerfully commit your life to growing in these areas.

During the Day

Look for ways today to express those characteristics you want to cultivate in your life.

Day Three: *Acting Our Way into Christ-likeness*

Yesterday, as a During the Day direction, I asked you to look for ways to express those characteristics of Christ-life you want to cultivate in your life. Did you find ways to do this? What happened?

* * *

It is an often ignored truth that we act our way into Christ-likeness. I've never seen persons who *studied* their way into Christ-likeness. Nor have I seen persons who *prayed* or *worshiped* their way into Christ-likeness. Yet, I've seen countless persons who *acted* their way into Christ-likeness. The likeness of Christ shines forth from their lives. All of them pray; many of them are people with a deep prayer life. They study to varying degrees. They worship. But most of all, they are people whose acts of mercy make the "look like" Jesus.

John Wesley set forth two categories of means of grace—channels through which God's grace is conveyed to use. These were *instituted* means of grace, or works of piety and *prudential* means of grace, or works of mercy. Instituted means of grace included prayer, scripture, the Lord's Supper, fasting, and Christian conferencing. Prudential means of grace or works of mercy were doing no harm and doing good.

Wesley believed, and I agree, that when we resist doing harm and when we do good, we are acting our way into Christ-likeness, and God's grace comes to us through this channel.

This is *being Christ,* living his life in the world. The world desperately needs it.

Mother Teresa has put her mental finger on the deepest need, not just of a people who are dying in the slums of Calcutta, but of all human beings. Not only has she defined the need, she has given herself and her Order of Serving Nuns, to be the answer to the need.

> In these twenty years of work amongst the people, I have come more and more to realize that it is *being unwanted* that is the worst disease that any human being can ever experience. (Think about that—being unwanted the worst disease.) Nowadays, we have found medicine for leprosy and lepers can be cured. There's medicine for TB and consumptives can be cured. For all kinds of diseases there are medicines and cures. But for being unwanted, except there are willing hands to serve and there's a loving heart to love, I don't think this terrible disease can ever be cured (Muggeridge, pp. 98–99).

Willing hands to serve and loving hearts to love—acting our way into Christ-likeness. James spoke a penetrating word about this. "What does it profit, my brethren, if a man says he has faith but has not works? Can his faith save him? If a brother or sister is ill-clad and in lack of daily food, and one of you says to them, 'Go in peace, be warmed and filled,' without giving them the things needed for the body, what does it profit? So faith by itself, if it has no works, is dead" (James 2: 14–17, RSV).

Reflecting and Recording

Go back to the list of persons you made on Day One of this week, persons in whom Christ is felt to live again. Reflect upon their lives in light of the means of grace John Wesley outlined: prayer, scripture, the Lord's Supper, fasting, Christian conferencing, doing no harm, and doing good. Were a number of these disciplines incorporated in their lives? Which were the most common?

In your observation did any of these persons act their way into Christ-likeness by doing no harm and doing good?

✻ ✻ ✻

During the Day

Continue to look for ways to express the characteristics of Christ-likeness you listed yesterday. Expressing these you will be acting your way into Christ-likeness.

Day Four: *What Christ Has Been and Done for Us*

In the first chapter of his Gospel, with almost breathtaking succinctness and rapidity, Mark tells the story of Jesus' forty days in the wilderness, his call and baptism, then his call of the disciples, and his beginning ministry in a series of healings. One of those healings was of a leper (Mark 1:40–45). In New Testament times, leprosy was the most dreaded of all diseases. The victim not only suffered physical debilitation, but also mental and emotional pain and anguish. Lepers were forced to live alone; they had to wear special clothing so others could identify them and avoid them. Perhaps the most abysmal humiliation was that they were required by law to announce vocally their despicable condition: *Unclean! Unclean!*

Mark tells of one of these lepers coming boldly to Jesus, kneeling before him and appealing, ''If you want to, you can make me clean.'' Then there is packed into one beautiful sentence almost everything Jesus was and was about. ''Jesus was filled with pity for him, and stretched out his hand and placed it on the leper, saying, 'Of course I want to—*be clean!* (Mark 1:41 Phillips). That tells it all! Stay with that encounter for a moment to get the full impact of it. By law the leper had no right to even draw near Jesus, much less speak to him. How, we do not know, but he knew that despite his repulsive disease, his grotesque appearance, Jesus would *see him,* really see him, and respond to him as a person, not as a maimed, disfigured piece of flesh. Note Jesus' response: he *listened,* he *looked* at him, and he *touched* him—the three action-responses that no one else would dare make.

I could have chosen more stories—Zacchaeus, the woman at the well, or others—that make the same point. But I deliberately share this one to make the point more graphically. If Jesus' ministry goes to the point of involving him with the poorest of the poor, the ugliest of the ugly, can there be any question that we must move through our days responding in affirming love and care to the persons whose lives intersect ours? (*AC,* pp. 139–40).

What Christ has been and done for us we must be and do for others. Our life in Christ and our ministry in his name are inseparable. A spirituality that does not lead to active ministry becomes an indulgent preoccupation with self which grieves the Holy Spirit and violates the presence of the indwelling Christ.

Reflecting and Recording

Jesus responded to the leper in three ways: he *listened* to him, he *looked* at him, and he *touched* him. These responses are essential if we are going to be for others what Christ has been for us.

Jesus *listened.* Is there anything that enhances feelings of worth more than being listened to?

Jesus *looked* at the leper. He gave the leper his attention. To look at and listen to another—to give attention in this fashion—communicates the love of Christ more than anything else.

Jesus *touched* the leper. The call of Jesus to us is to be involved, not to be aloof.

List two or three people who need to be given the attention Jesus would give, people whom you know who need love and care.

1._____

2._____

3._____

Make some notes below each name about how you might be to these persons what Christ has been for you.

During the Day

Set about deliberately *being Christ* to the persons listed above. But also remember that Christ's presence is shared spontaneously, even with strangers. As we grow vividly alive in Christ, his Spirit is expressed through us. The fantastic and thrilling rubric for our lives can become a viable possibility: *We will be Christ to and/or receive Christ from every person we meet.*

On page 173 there is a tent card with the inscription, "What Christ has been and done for us we must be and do for others." Cut out, fold, and put it in a place where you will see it often during the next few days.

Day Five: *Being Christ by Forgiving*

Yesterday we considered the dramatic encounter of Jesus with a leper. From that encounter we learned about how we are to respond as Christ to others. He *listened,* he *looked,* and he *touched.* He was always an affirming presence and likewise must we be. Today we continue our emphasis on our call: *What Christ has been and done for us we must be and do for others.*

We focus here on one of the most desperate needs—the need for forgiveness.

The most graphic story of Jesus' ministry of forgiveness is that of the woman caught in the act of adultery and brought to Jesus.

They went each to his own house, but Jesus went to the Mount of Olives. Early in the morning he came again to the temple; all the people came to him, and he sat down and taught them. The scribes and the Pharisees brought a woman who had been caught in adultery, and placing her in the midst they said to him, "Teacher, this woman has been caught in the act of adultery. Now in the law Moses commanded us to stone such. What do you say about her?" This they said to test him, that they might have some charge to bring against him. Jesus bent down and wrote with his finger on the ground. And as they continued to ask him, he stood up and said to them, "Let him who is without sin among you be the first to throw a stone at her." And once more he bent down and wrote with his finger on the ground. But when they heard it, they went away, one by one, beginning with the eldest, and Jesus was left alone with the woman standing before him. Jesus looked up and said to her, "Woman, where are they? Has no one condemned you?" She said, "No one, Lord." And Jesus said, "Neither do I condemn you; go, and do not sin again.

—John 8:1–11, RSV

My father has little formal education, but he is a very wise man. Recently we were talking about this story of the woman accused of adultery and brought to Jesus for condemnation. That mysterious act of Jesus—writing in the dirt—came up. What did Jesus write? That question will continue to puzzle us, but Dad had an intriguing idea: Perhaps what Jesus wrote was a question—"What if this woman were your daughter? Or sister?"

That does make the issue penetratingly personal, doesn't it? No matter what he wrote, we know it took only a look, a call for the *sinless* to cast the first stone, then a word written in the sand, to send the accusers slinking away. And Jesus was left alone with the woman. In a few seconds she learned what she had been seeking all her shameful life—what it really means to love and be loved. It had come in the presence of venomous and stony hearts, when death was only a pile of stones away. The accusers were gone, but the woman was not yet free. Then it came, the transforming word: "Neither do I condemn you; go and sin no more."

Affirmation was there, yes. Affirmation acted out in forgiveness. And that forgiveness brought healing. That's who Christ is, and what Christ has been and done for us, we must be and do for others.

There is a troubling word of Jesus recorded in John 20:23: "If you forgive the sins of any, they are forgiven; if you retain the sins of any, they are retained." There are depths of mystery here that we may never plumb, but that gives us no excuse. The onus is upon us, and it should be an exhilarating not a depressing responsibility. We can understand at least this: We are to be the channels of Christ's forgiving grace; and if we aren't, there may be those who will not experience the joyful meaning of that forgiveness.

We can be those channels in a lot of ways, not least of which is *nonjudgmental listening*. Such listening requires a humility on my part, and an honest recognition that I am never immune to "falling," that no matter how *secure* I may be in my present "walk with the Lord" I may slip and stumble, and fall into snares as damaging and destructive as those about which I am hearing from another who has honored me by sharing his or her confession. If I enter a relationship, or listen to a confession more intent on *curing* than *caring* I will not be a channel of Christ's forgiving love. If I care I will listen nonjudgmentally.

We must also *announce* the good news of forgiveness. A primary function of a priest—and all of us as Christians are priests—is to say the word: "In the name of Christ you are forgiven." I have seen it over and over again: persons who have been earnest and sincere in their prayer for forgiveness, and who are themselves forgiving persons, yet cannot get relief for their own guilt; they are not assured of Christ's forgiveness. Then the word is spoken by another Christian, "you are forgiven," and that does it—they know and can accept forgiveness and freedom from guilt. Release and relief comes to others when we are given the grace to hear their confession and take the authority to announce, "In the name of Christ, you are forgiven" (*AC*, pp. 143–44).

Reflecting and Recording

Two things stand out in Jesus' response to the woman and her accusers. First, the privilege of judgment belongs to God not to us. None of us is without sin, so how can we prescribe judgment for others? Second, our response to persons who have made mistakes and/or sinned should be concern—pity in the best sense of the word. That means that our first effort in relation to sin is merciful action for redemption, not punishment for retaliation.

Love and forgiveness is the only power that can break the cycle of sin and evil. Neville Ward has spoken this challenging word: "Those who break (the) chain of resentment, retaliation, violence, and hostility are people who take away the sins of the world."

Spend some time thinking about how you need to be for others what Christ has been for you as a forgiving presence. Is there one situation in which you can act specifically in the next few days?

✳ ✳ ✳

During the Day

In the discussion about forgiveness, I mentioned two ways for us to be channels for Christ's forgiving grace: nonjudgemental listening and announcing the good news of forgiveness. Look for ways to be such a channel today.

Day Six: *Solidarity with the Poor*

In her book, *The Eighth Day of Creation*, Elizabeth O'Connor tells of an experience of St. Francis de Sales.

> St. Francis de Sales was once approached by a disciple who said to him, "Sir, you speak so much about the love of God, but you never tell us how to achieve it. Won't you tell me how one comes to love God?" And St. Francis replied, "There is only one way and that is to love Him."
>
> "But you don't quite understand my question. What I asked was, 'how do you engender this love of God?'" And St. Francis said, "By loving Him."
>
> Once again the pupil came back with the same question, "But what steps do you take? Just what do you do in order to come into the possession of this love?" And all St. Francis said was, "You begin by loving and you go on loving and loving teaches you how to love. And the more you love, the more you learn to love." (O'Connor, p. 66–67)

The characteristic element of the Christ-life is love expressed as compassion. The epistle of James says it clearly. "If a brother or sister is ill-clad and in lack of daily food, and one of you says to them, 'Go in peace, be warmed and filled,' without giving them the things needed for the body, what does it profit? . . . You see that a man is justified by works and not by faith alone. . . . For as the body apart from the spirit is dead, so faith apart from works is dead" (James 2:15–16, 24, 26, RSV).

Jesus' warning about the Last Judgment makes the point scathingly clear. "Then the King will say to those at his right hand, 'Come, O blessed of my Father, inherit the kingdom prepared for you from the foundation of the world; for I was hungry and you gave me food, I was thirsty and you gave me drink, I was a stranger and you welcomed me, I was naked and you clothed me, I was sick and you visited me, I was in prison and you came to me' " (Matt. 25:34–36, RSV).

One of the most important signs of compassion is our commitment and efforts to be in *solidarity with the poor.* Matthew Fox, whose book, *A Spirituality Named Compassion* (Winston Press, 1971), I heartily recommend, says that "compassion is not knowing about the suffering and pain of others. It is, in some way, knowing that pain, entering into it, sharing it and tasting it insofar as possible." We are not simply called to know that others suffer, or to assess the painful situations in which they may be, we are to feel the other's feelings. And not only feel the other's feeling, but act on behalf of the other."

This is at least a part of what it means to be in *solidarity with the poor and oppressed of the world.*

Reflecting and Recording

To introduce and focus only for one day on such a big idea as solidarity with the poor may be unfair. Being Christ in the world is a call demanding a lifetime response. But I hope that all the issues raised in this workbook will provide some signals for our Christ-life journey.

There are at least three ports by which to enter into solidarity with the poor.

Direct action. This is what James called us to and what Jesus said would be the basis for our judgment. Go back and read those scripture passages.

✳ ✳ ✳

Stewardship. I control the way I spend my money, and I make the decision as to how I will use the resources that are mine. By responsible Christian stewardship I can enter into solidarity with the poor.

Prayer.

Prayer then, especially intercession, is an expression of our greatest love and is a gateway to solidarity. Instead of keeping pain away from us, loving prayer leads us into the suffering of God and of others. The deeper our love of God, the more we will suffer. The more we suffer, the more we will pray.

Our suffering and the suffering of others is embraced by the compassionate Christ, in a way that we may never fully understand; our intercession, through identity with suffering, becomes a channel of Christ's liberating power (*AC,* p. 156).

Think about the above ports of entry into solidarity with the poor. Think of one specific way you can begin to express compassion. An example. My wife and I are tithers. We give 10 percent of our income to the church. Four years ago we made the decision to support a child through the Christian Children's Fund—not a part of our tithe. Two years ago we decided to tithe our house payment. We give 10 percent of the amount of our house payment, not a part of our tithe, to Habitat for Humanity to provide housing for the poor. Occasionally I, and often my wife, work on the actual building of these houses. We are constantly driven to confession of and deep penitence for our failure to be in solidarity with the poor, but we are consciously working on it and finding meaning and joy.

Make a decision now about one way you will begin to express solidarity with the poor, perhaps using the ports of entry discussed above. Write that commitment here.

During the Day

Take some initial step in acting out the commitment you have just made.

Day Seven: *The Style of a Servant*

One of the most beautiful and descriptive words about Jesus is found in Philippians 2:5–22:

Let this mind be in you which was also in Christ Jesus, who, being in the form of God, did not consider equality with God something to be grasped, but emptied himself by taking the form of a servant, and coming in the likeness of men. And being found in appearance as a man, He humbled Himself and became obedient to the point of death, even the death of the cross. Therefore God also has highly exalted Him and given Him the name which is above every name, that at the name of Jesus every knee should bow, of those in heaven, and of those on earth, and of those under the earth, and that every tongue should confess that Jesus Christ is Lord, to the glory of God the father (NKJV).

Not only is this a vivid description of Jesus, it is a call to us. "*Let this mind be in you,* which was also in Christ Jesus . . . [who took] the form of a servant." But not many of us want to be servants, do we? Yet, it is clear as we read the New Testament that this was the most distinctive quality of Jesus' style of ministry. And Jesus leaves little doubt that it is the style to which he calls us. "The disciple is not superior to his teacher, nor the slave to his master" (Matt. 10:24, JB). "Anyone who wants to be great among you must be your servant . . . just as the Son of Man came not to be served but to serve" (Matt. 20:26–28, JB). Not only does Jesus call us to this style, he gives us life through this style: "Anyone who finds his life will lose it; anyone who loses his life for my sake will find it" (Matt. 10:39, JB).

To get in touch with Jesus' call, note this: *There is a vast difference between the way most of us serve and Jesus' call to be a servant.*

The way most of us serve keeps us in control. We choose whom, when, where, and how we will serve. We stay in charge. Jesus is calling for something else. He is calling us to be servants. When we make this choice, we give up the right to be in charge. The amazing thing is that when we make this choice we experience great freedom. We become available and vulnerable, and we lose our fear of being stepped on, or manipulated, or taken advantage of. Are not these our basic fears? We do not want to be in a position of weakness (*AC*, p. 150).

We close our Alive in Christ journey by underlining this call of Jesus to be a servant, after his style. This requires giving up the right to be in control. When we make this decision and give up this right, we experience freedom. Strength, vitality, joy, and meaning are ours when we choose a lifestyle of servanthood, rather than serving now and then as we please. It is then that Christ lives in us forcefully, and we communicate his presence vividly to others.

In talking about his longing for Christ to come alive in his friends in Galatia, Paul used the image of giving birth to a child. "Oh, my dear children, I feel the pangs of childbirth all over again till Christ be formed within you" (Gal. 4:19 Phillips). Rachel Richardson Smith reflected on the meaning of the Incarnation in light of her own pregnancy and giving birth. She said,

In pregnancy a woman's body takes over. . . . I felt as though I had lost control of my body. It went ahead on its own and left me in shock somewhere behind. . . . In pregnancy I became one with my body as at no other time in my life.

She went on to speak of a woman's being intricately bound up with the new person within her, even though distinct from it. "The two are one," she says,

and herein lies the paradox. The pregnant woman is both herself and this other being. The two are distinct from each other, though they are not separate.
This too is the paradox of incarnation. . . . God is both Christ and other than Christ. Though not separate from Christ, God is distinct from Christ. . . . Christ is not all of God, as the newborn baby is not all of the mother. But in Christ, God gives birth to God. (*The Christian Century,* Dec. 19, 1979)

We may extend the use of that image for our life in Christ, for in us the Incarnation continues. I am not all of Christ, even as the newborn baby is not all of the mother, and even as Jesus Christ is not all of God. But by an incomprehensible work of grace, Christ is alive in me, and to the degree of my yieldedness to his indwelling presence, I live Christ's life, and I can be Christ to others (*AC*, pp. 158–59).

Reflecting and Recording

Since this is the last day of your workbook, sit as long as you can reflecting on this seven-week, Alive-in-Christ Journey. Put down some words or sentences that communicate what you have experienced, questions that have been raised, decisions you have made, directions you have found, truth that has come alive. This is only for you, so make notes that will speak to you, perhaps, a few months from now when you review what you have written here and on the next page.

During the Day

Make a decision now that, as within you lies the power and with the Lord as your helper, from this point on each day you will seek to be Christ to and/or receive Christ from every person you meet.

Group Meeting for Week Seven

Note: The leader for this week should bring a chalkboard or newsprint to the meeting. Read No. 3 of Sharing Together.

Introduction

This is the last meeting designed for this group. You may have already talked about the possibility of continuing to meet. You should conclude those plans. Some groups find it meaningful to select two or three weeks of the workbook and go through those weeks again as an extension of time together. Others continue for an additional set time, using other resources.

Whatever you choose to do, it is usually helpful to determine the actual time line in order that persons can make clear commitment.

Another possibility that has been very effective in our congregation in Memphis is for one or two persons to decide they will recruit and lead a group of new persons through the workbook. Many people are looking for a small group growth experience, and this is a way to respond to that need.

Sharing Together

1. Begin your sharing by allowing each person to share his/her most meaningful and most difficult days of this week's involvement with the workbook.

2. On Day One each person was asked to name three persons "in whom Christ is felt to live again." Ask each person in the group to take from one to two minutes to talk about one of the persons they named. Who is (or was) she? What is he like? How is she like Christ?

3. Now ask everyone to look at the list of words used to describe these persons during their Reflecting and Recording on Day One. Leader, write these words on a chalkboard or newsprint as they are called out by each person. After the first person calls out his/her words, the leader should put a check each time a word is repeated. Note the dominant characteristics of persons in whom Christ is felt to live again.

4. Ask anyone who followed through with the During the Day suggestion on Day One to share the results.

5. On Day Three we focused on acting our way into Christ-likeness. Spend five to ten minutes discussing this in light of the characteristics you listed of persons "in whom Christ is felt to live again."

6. Take some time to talk about solidarity with the poor as discussed on Day Seven, and ask as many as will to share the decisions they have made to enter into solidarity with the poor. Is there some symbolic act the group could share?

7. Use the balance of your discussion time (save time for prayer) for persons to share the meaning of this seven-week journey, questions they have, insights they have received, changes that have occurred, commitments they have made.

Praying Together

1. Begin your time of prayer by asking each person to express gratitude to God in a two- or three-sentence prayer for something significant that has happened to him/her as a result of these seven weeks.

2. Give each person the opportunity to share whatever decision or commitment he or she has made, or will make, to an ongoing life in Christ. Be specific. Follow each person's verbalizing of these decisions and commitments by having some other person in the group offer a brief prayer of thanksgiving and support for this person.

3. A benediction is a blessing or greeting shared with another or by a group in parting. The "passing of the peace" is such a benediction.

You take a person's hand, look into his or her eyes and say, "The peace of God be with you," and the person responds, "And may God's peace be yours." Then that person, taking the hands of the person next to him or her, says 'The peace of God be with you," and receives the response, "And may God's peace by yours." Standing in a circle, let the leader "pass the peace," and let it go around the circle.

4. Having completed the passing of the peace, speak to one another in a more spontaneous way. Move about to different persons in the group, saying whatever you feel is appropriate for your parting blessing to each person. Or, you may simply embrace the person and say nothing. In your own unique way, "bless" each person who has shared this journey with you.

Notes

Sources quoted in this workbook are identified in the text by author and page number. If more than one work by the same author is cited, the title of the work is included in the citation. Bibliographic information for each source is listed below.

Dunnam, Maxie. *Alive in Christ*. Nashville: Abingdon, 1982.

———. *The Communicator's Commentary: Galatians, Ephesians, Philippians, Colossians, Philemon* (Vol. VIII). Waco, TX: Word, 1982.

Glasser, William, *Take Effective Control of Your Life*. New York: Harper & Row, 1984.

Muggeridge, Malcolm. *Something Beautiful for God*. London: William Collins, 1971.

Nouwen, Henri J. M. *Sojourners*, June 13, 1981.

O'Connor, Elizabeth. *The Eighth Day of Creation*. Waco, *TX: Word, 1971.*

Parke, John H. "How to Pray for Healing" *in Sharing Magazine,* July, 1973.

Stewart, James. *A Man in Christ*. Grand Rapids: Baker Books, 1975.

Willimon, William H. *The Gospel for the Person Who Has Everything.* Valley Forge, PA: Judson, 1978.

Spiritual formation is that dynamic process of receiving through faith and appropriating through commitment, discipline and action, the living Christ into our own life to the end that our life will conform to, and manifest the reality of Christ's presence in the world.

Spiritual formation is that dynamic process of receiving through faith and appropriating through commitment, discipline and action, the living Christ into our own life to the end that our life will conform to, and manifest the reality of Christ's presence in the world.

To love and accept on the basis of worthiness is not worthy of being called love and acceptance.

To love and accept on the basis of worthiness is not worthy of being called love and acceptance.

There is in the Christian experience of salvation a discontinuity between what was and what now is.

There is in the Christian experience of salvation a discontinuity between what was and what now is.

What Christ has been and done for us we must be and do for others.

What Christ has been and done for us we must be and do for others.